Contents

Editorial

Where Architects Fear to Tread …

A softly softly approach to development is now a given for architects. The sensitivity to materials, context and scale that has come to be equated with sustainability is now established and institutionalised via legislation and government directives. But what if the means by which we are pursuing the Holy Grail of sustainability is too piecemeal, too tentative and too slow?

Could we simply be failing to provide accommodation for future generations?

This title of Δ may not be to the taste of all our readers. The fact that we are raising the spectre that building prefabricated structures on a greater scale might be preferable to designing diminutive bespoke constructions may in itself seem to be detestable and fly against the very heart of architectural creation. Many architects may simply not want to learn from the lessons of the Wal-Mart mega-shed. But what is truly invaluable here is the fact that guest-editors Ian Abley and Jonathan Schwinge have dared to raise their heads above the parapet and contest what has now come to be received knowledge and an increasingly accepted way of talking and going about things.

The vision of the modular megastructure may seem, at first, to belong to another, earlier age. The words of Buckminster Fuller and Reyner Banham are, indeed, repeatedly invoked throughout the issue. Ian Abley juxtaposes postwar Britain with the work of the Japanese Metabolists; Jayne Merkel provides an insightful exploration into the work of Eero Saarinen; and Stanley Mathews discusses the work of Cedric Price within the context of postwar social and economic trends. What these architects all share in common is a boldness of vision and conception that emanates a human optimism, which is now a complete anathema in the 21st century. Any faith in human progress in architecture being well and truly toppled by the 1970s with the perceived failure of Modernism and the popular disdain for the poorly produced systems building of public housing schemes that were epitomised by the tower block.

But could our timidity in terms of the built environment also be a product of a wider lack of human self-belief? Have we lost our faith in 'the manmade', and now believe that we can only move forward if it is in some way imitative or harnessed to nature? Is it possible that by not asserting our potential, at this very crucial point in time, to find real solutions to large-scale problems such as the demise of fossil fuel and global warming at the level of the megastructure, we could be merely dabbling too late? *Helen Castle*

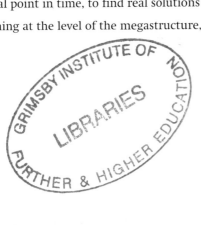

Jonathan Schwinge, Cloud Piercer, proposal for mile-high megastructures in the Thames Estuary, 2005.

Introduction

Things Will Endure Less Than Us

Ian Abley challenges the current architectural veneration of everything small and tailormade. Could a correlation between the small scale and the sustainable be entirely misplaced? Could our very predilection for 'sensitive' diminuitive design be causing us to completely overlook the potential of the megastructure? Shouldn't we be striving to deliver reusable spaces with recyclable parts to the greatest number of people?

How might architecture and engineering meet the challenges of a world of 8.3 billion people within the next quarter of a century?

It is already clear how that population might be clothed by 2030. Editing this text in the first week of September 2005, top-quality and highly affordable Chinese clothing was being blocked from import into Europe by Peter Mandelson, the European Commissioner for External Trade, who simultaneously insisted that 'the benefits of free and fair trade should be extended to all, especially the poorest'.[1] Decoded, this means free trade for Chinese manufacturers is considered unfair, despite European retailers and their customers wanting the produce.

European Commissioner for External Trade, Peter Mandelson (left) and the Chinese Minister of Commerce, Bo Xilai, in the middle of a trade war over the production of clothes, Shanghai, China, 10 June 2005.

Imagine if such productive powers were put to work in the manufacture of top-quality and affordable architecture for UK retailers to sell to the buying public. Think of IKEA x Chinese manufacturing capacity and imagine an international trade dispute in construction.

Of course, such a scenario seems remote, but not for technical reasons. It is entirely possible to imagine architectural products made anywhere in the world to be installed on site, whether singly or stacked up, or installed into a prepared infrastructure as manufactured land. Most people think that land is a finite resource. This is certainly the

REYNER BANHAM

Megastructure

'Megastructure, the concept of a giant, adaptable, multi-purpose building containing most of the functions of a city, was one of the dominant design themes of the late 1950s and most of the 1960s, occupying the difficult middle ground between architecture and town planning. Vast, it offered architects the chance to create super-monuments on a scale matching the modern city; adaptable, it offered the citizenry the possibility of creating their own small-scale environments within the enormous frame. Yet in spite of these promises, architects and citizens alike had abandoned the idea and sought more modest solutions to their needs – and ambitions – soon after 1970.' In the flyleaf to his fascinating *Megastructure: Urban Futures of the Recent Past* (1976), Reyner Banham notes the loss of confidence by professional and public alike. Yet megastructure may once again be a way we might make sense of the megalopolis.

presumption behind *British Planning Policy Guidance 3: Housing*.[2] But a megastructure creates more land as a serviced platform, either with an all-weather envelope divorced from the accommodation, or relying on the accommodation modules to deal with the climate. Modules are best as finished volumes, or maybe kits of panels, frames and components requiring a greater degree of fit, but with the anticipation that they will wear out, become obsolete and need replacing from the latest catalogues.

Unfortunately the prospect that the Chinese might manufacture architecture as modules or modular megastructures for export seems remote, mostly because the UK would resist the imports through the obstacle of the planning system. Yet we are used to commercial offices, shopping malls or hospitals being modest single-use structures capable of refit. Meanwhile, the stock of single-family, site-built dwellings in town and throughout suburbia has accommodated change better than attempts, from the 1950s to the 1970s, at distinctly nonmegastructural residential system building.

The question remains: Why can't architecture be better manufactured for modular upgrade through an international division of labour capable of sustaining megastructures?

Megastructure: Urban Futures of the Recent Past was written 30 years ago by Reyner Banham on the assumption that, in his foreseeable future, after the Pompidou Centre in Paris, they would no longer be built. Ultimately, he said, megastructures were a 'self-cancelling concept' in attempting to architecturally order flexibility in use over time.[3] This is a flawed but still more convincing explanation for the no-show of megastructures than that given by Colin Davies in *The Prefabricated Home*. There, megastructuralism is dismissed as *Blade Runner* territory, and for the 'vertiginous nightmare of the environment it creates'.[4] Banham had instead begun with an almost boringly practical description of megastructures from Ralph Wilcoxon, the planning librarian at the College of Environmental Design, Berkeley:

- constructed of modular units
- capable of great or even 'unlimited' extension
- a structural framework into which smaller structural units (for example, rooms, houses, or small buildings of other sorts) can be built – or even 'plugged-in' or 'clipped-on' after having been prefabricated elsewhere
- a structural framework expected to have a useful life much longer than that of the smaller units which it might support.[5]

This is more about accommodating change than about size, as Rem Koolhaas and Bruce Mau struggled with in *S,M,L,XL*.[6] For Banham, over the period of residential system building, megastructures 'were all large buildings – but not

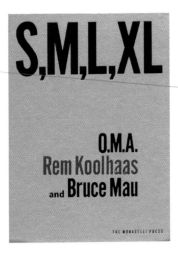

put the challenge very clearly in *Nine Chains to the Moon*, as early as 1938:

> The goal is the emergence of humanity.
> The means is industrial. Not re-form, but to form.
> In architecture 'form' is a noun; in industry, 'form' is a verb. Industry is concerned with DOING, whereas architecture has been engrossed with making replicas of end results of what people have industrially demonstrated in the past.[10]

In 1938 the world population was over 2 billion. In 2006, just under 6.5 billion people equate to over 27 human chains to the moon. By 2030 nearly 36 human chains will represent the 8.3 billion of us. Four times the humanity that Fuller considered less than a century earlier. What if we were all the demanding customers of manufacturers intent on forming the environment on an industrial scale? Such a prospect seems alarming in the UK, where everyone from the government down hopes that the property market in ageing and insufficient housing will not crash. A country where 'sustainable communities', the big idea from the Office of the Deputy Prime Minister, is both stuck in the 'small is beautiful' mode of thinking following EF Schumacher[11] and has, under John Prescott, encouraged the nonsense that architectural form determines social behaviour.[12]

In the last year, and in contrast to the meanness of the British discussion, it has been reassuring to read the Fulleresque ambition of Bruce Mau[13] and the Institute without Boundaries,[14] with their 'Massive Change' project.[15] They recognise that optimism about development runs counter to the mood of the times. In that spirit, this issue of *Δ* offers a number of arguments, to be pursued into 2006 on www.audacity.org. Uncertain about what the countryside is for, confused about biomimicry, and with an exaggerated sense that development remains a source of social vulnerability, Mau's further publications in 2006 will be worth engaging with. In all other regards he seems to see a potentially bright industrial future.

However, to avoid adopting Fuller's technocratic approach it is necessary to recognise there are social factors that are beyond the designer's professional ability to resolve. Sixty years before Mandelson challenged China over clothing production, the atomic bomb was dropped on the inhabitants of Hiroshima at 8.15 am on 6 September 1945. That megastructural thinking was best articulated by the postwar generation of Japanese architects demonstrates how technical possibilities might be a response to wider limitations, but cannot escape their social context. September 2005 saw the senseless loss of life in the New Orleans flooding following hurricane Katrina. The US failure to invest in structural flood defences, and the cynical abandonment of the poorest of New Orleans stands as an indictment. This coincided with the anniversary of the attack on the New York World Trade Center

all large buildings of the time were megastructures'.[7] He relied upon Fumihiko Maki's definition of 'megastructure'[8] as 'a large frame into which all the functions of a city or part of a city are housed'. Maki continued that such a structural approach has 'been made possible by present day technology', and that megastructures are 'a manmade feature of the landscape'.[9]

The megastructuralists knew the citizens needed to upgrade and modify their parts of the city according to technological advances and social circumstance, while the economies of scale of infrastructural investment needed to be pushed, literally, to new heights. Buckminster Fuller had

'Urbanization, one of humankind's most successful and ambitious programs, is the triumph of the unnatural over the natural, the grid over the organic. We remain committed to a global program of extrusion upward and repetition outward in an effort to provide shelter that is safe, healthy, and uplifting. Underway on a scale never before witnessed, one side effect of urbanization is the liberation of vast depopulated territories for the efficient production of "nature". Bruce Mau, *Massive Change* (2004).

on 11 September 2001. Then, anti-capitalist sentiment tended to apologise for the terrorist atrocity, as if ordinary Americans 'had it coming' for living in the world's richest country. In 2005 environmentalists helped apologise for the lack of preparedness in New Orleans, arguing against development in flood plains at a time of climate change.

It is important to appreciate that technical problems are always approached through the prevailing ideology, and today all development is seen as a problem for nature, not as a solution for man. Architectural and engineering responses are never value free. Yet there is no need to elide politics and economics with technique and aesthetics as Koolhaas manages in *Content*.[16] Sure, capitalism has limits, but construction has not begun to push them, and they are not natural. The long-running international retreat from the task of advancing architecture and engineering, including the abandonment of megastructural thinking, dressed up these days as concern for the environment, is no serious anti-capitalism. It is another apology for the lack of dynamic at home, and a resistance to the gains in production being made abroad.

Nor is there a need to reject the perfectibility of consumer products, as Mau seems too prepared for.[17] It is possible to design temporarily optimal modules to fit into extendable infrastructures with a far longer design life.[18] Such an approach is also necessary, because as the Futurist Antonio Sant'Elia perfectly expressed in 1914, 'things will endure less than us. Every generation must build its own city.'[19] This tends to mean a disruptive tearing-down of the composition of cities. In contrast, the megastructure brings method and economies of scale to the processes of architecturally replacing and recycling that which is exhausted, and to reusing that which is still an extendable investment.

Koolhaas and Mau appreciate that architectural production must serve a mass market, and so it remains to be seen whether Banham was premature in declaring the death of megastructural thinking. Thinking that might be the manufactured antidote to small-minded sustainability. For as the latest UN Habitat report *Financing Urban Shelter* appreciated, 'by 2030, an additional 3 billion people – about 40% of the global population – will need housing. That means theoretically completing 96,150 housing units a day, starting now.'[20]

Is this need for massive change in architectural production something the 2006 Venice Biennale will seriously consider? The theme of the 10th International Architecture Exhibition from September to November is the 'meta-city', or 'an agglomeration that extends beyond the traditional form and concept of the city, that has come to exceed traditional boundaries, defining new issues and needs concerning its governance, and undergoing profound transformations in the composition of its population, and in its working habits'.[21] We shall see what that means under the direction of Professor Ricky Burdett.[22] ⌂

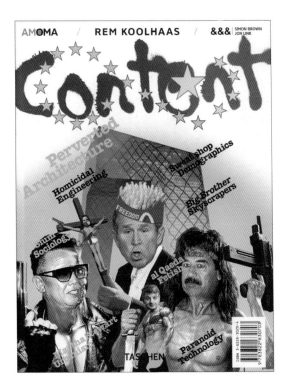

Notes

1. Peter Mandelson, 'Towards a more open rules-based trade, for the benefit of all', http://europa.eu.int/comm/commission_barroso/mandelson/index_en.htm, accessed 28 August 2005.
2. Office of the Deputy Prime Minister, *Government's Response to the Environment, Transport and Regional Affairs: Seventeenth Report – Planning Policy Guidance 3: Housing Cm 4667*, TSO (LONDON), 2000. www.odpm.gov.uk/stellent/groups/odpm_planning/documents/page/odpm_plan_606933.hcsp.
3. Reyner Banham, *Megastructure: Urban Futures of the Recent Past*, Thames and Hudson (London), 1976, p 216.
4. Colin Davies, *The Prefabricated Home*, Reaktion Books (London), 2005, p 41.
5. Ralph Wilcoxon, quoted in Reyner Banham, op cit, p 8.
6. Rem Koolhaas and Bruce Mau, *S,M,L,XL*, Monacelli Press (New York), 1995, reprinted 1997.
7. Reyner Banham, op cit, p 7.
8. Ibid, p 8.
9. Fumihiko Maki, *Investigations in Collective Form*, Washington University School of Architecture (St Louis, MO), 1964, p 8. http://library.wustl.edu/units/spec/archives/photos/maki/maki-entire.pdf, accessed 24 July 2005.
10. Richard Buckminster Fuller, *Nine Chains to the Moon*, Anchor Books, Doubleday (New York), 1971, p 41.
11. EF Schumacher, *Small Is Beautiful: Study of Economics as If People Mattered*, Vintage (London), 1993, first published by Blond and Briggs Ltd, 1973.
12. www.odpm.gov.uk, accessed 6 September 2005.
13. www.brucemaudesign.com, accessed 25 August 2005.
14. www.institutewithoutboundaries.com, accessed 25 August 2005.
15. Bruce Mau with Jennifer Leonard and the Institute without Boundaries, *Massive Change*, Phaidon (London and New York), 2004.
16. Rem Koolhaas, *Content*, Taschen (London), 2004.
17. Bruce Mau, interview, 'Danish Design is Slumbering', part of *Too Perfect – Seven New Denmarks*, September 2004. www.tooperfect.dk.
18. Yona Friedman, *Toward a Scientific Architecture*, MIT Press, 1975.
19. Antonio Sant'Elia, 'The Manifesto of Futurist Architecture', *Lacerba* (Florence), 1 August 1914, in Umbro Apollonio (ed), *Futurist Manifestos*, Museum of Fine Arts Publications (Boston, MA), 2001, pp 160–72.
20. United Nations Habitat, *Financing Urban Shelter – Global Report on Human Settlements 2005*, UN Habitat (Nairobi, Kenya), 2005. www.unhabitat.org/global_report_on_human_settlements_2005.asp, accessed 24 September 2005.
21. www.labiennale.org/en/index.html, accessed 26 September 2005.
22. www.lse.ac.uk/Depts/Cities, accessed 26 September 2005.

Beyond Little Britain

Ian Abley juxtaposes the demise of big architecture in 'Little Britain' with the ideas of the Metabolist movement in Japan, which grasped the potential of the large scale to 'reflect dynamic reality'.

Big suburbia is hated regardless of the fact that most British households live in suburbia. No fan of sprawling sameness, Peter Davey of the *Architectural Review* is also typical in his worries about the impact of big architecture on the composition of cities in this 'machine age'[1] – the phrase Reyner Banham used to describe the first machine age of ambitious Modernist architectural thought and limited practice from 1900 to 1930.[2] That period was the avant-garde prehistory of the functionalist Congrès Internationaux d'Architecture Moderne (CIAM), which Le Corbusier commanded from its inception in 1928, but which collapsed around its 10th congress between 1955 and 1959. It was Kenzo Tange who then stepped up with, as Dennis Sharp noted in his obituary in 2005, a new interest in 'flexibility, growth, change and indeterminacy'.[3]

Tange introduced the work of the young 'Metabolists' Kiyonori Kikutake[4] and Kisho Kurokawa,[5] who advocated an architecture that was adaptable to social and technological change. They had been seeing enough upheaval and reconstruction in Japan. CIAM had criticised the formalism of the schools of architecture, but after the Second World War and as early as CIAM VIII, hosted in 1951 at Hoddesdon, England, the year of the Festival of Britain, the possibility of total urban design was increasingly questioned. Not that surprising as Europe had also emerged from total war, and with the professional enthusiasm for comprehensive planning

having interwar origins. Pop Art was under way,[6] as were the divisive uncertainties of the Cold War.

Architectural confidence was shaking before planning really got going in Britain, which happened on 1 July 1948, when the Town and Country Planning Act 1947 nationalised development rights separate from the freehold ownership of land. This statute, made politically acceptable to farmers by the introduction of a regulated market for their produce as a continuation of rationing, was a deliberate attempt to prevent the unplanned ability of small builders and individual families building suburban homes on economically redundant farmland along the existing road network.[7] The train, bicycle and, most decisively, the car, made it possible for farmers to sell land piecemeal to subsidise their ailing businesses to commuters able to live remote from places of work.[8]

Planning killed the market for the prefabricated kit homes that some construction product manufacturers were innovating over the interwar period. It particularly ended the 'bungaloid growth' that had augmented the output of volume housebuilders up to the outbreak of another war. After that, and the brief period of emergency prefabs, house building was to be planned by the welfare state. Communities were to be designed by professionals, who were no longer united in CIAM. The Metabolists were marginal at CIAM, where a new generation of determinists, with Peter Smithson as a leading figure in Team X, the 10th congress organisers, trying to reinvigorate the conceit that architects could design communities. With the architectural profession in self-obsessed theoretical disarray, popular criticism of the mediocrity of system building was easy to indulge in. Community activists favouring refurbishment of Georgian and Victorian housing stock could applaud Old Labour as it pulled the plug on government underfunding of system building, increasingly from 1968 onwards. They could also applaud the turn of the planning system to ever wider public consultation as further interference with the freeholder's interests.

In contrast to the very British architectural profession's collapse into planning consultation, Kikutake had argued in 1965 that 'contemporary architecture must be metabolic. With the static theory of unsophisticated functionalism, it is impossible to discover functional changes. In order to reflect dynamic reality ... we must stop thinking about function and form, and think instead in terms of space and changeable function ... to serve free human living.'[9] This was hot, but still marginal, stuff. Architects interested in technology, like Archigram and the young Richard Rogers, were inspired by the design approach of the Metabolists and, notably, Kurokawa, against whom Rogers was later competing for the Pompidou Centre between 1968 and 1971.

Rogers was also attuned to community activism. In a fudge of the post-CIAM mood of determinist thought and the desire for public participation in design, Rogers today insists that buildings, properly composed in cities, will sustain community.

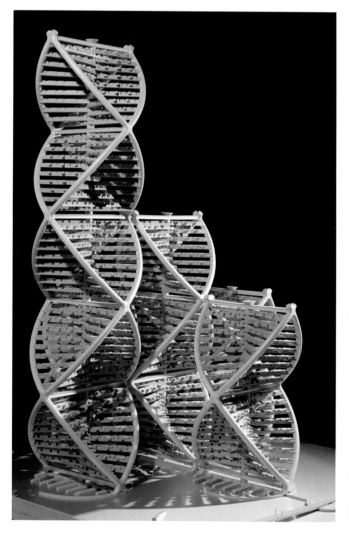

Kisho Kurokawa, photographed in 2005 by Koichi Inakoshi.

Kisho Kurokawa, Helix City, Tokyo, 1961
This is an urban megastructure to be developed both vertically and horizontally. Reminiscent of the structure of deoxyribonucleic acid (DNA) discovered in 1953, the helical structure acts as a 3-D cluster system linked to the city's transport systems.

Kisho Kurokawa, Floating City, Kasumigaura, 1961
Prepared with plans for the Tokyo International Airport at Narita, the roof-top transport systems are linked by spiral escalators through the structure to the harbour moorings at their base, and to each level. The residents build using all manners of construction, and with terraces, on the manmade land.

The winning scheme for the Pompidou Centre by Rogers, his then partner Renzo Piano, and the great engineer Peter Rice of Ove Arup and Partners, was a megastructure in the Paris composition of blocks, stacked double-height to leave one of the grids clear for a public piazza. It opened early in 1977 and was a design, as Philip Jodidio says in his gorgeous and inquiring *Piano*, that owed much to the ideas of Cedric Price and Joan Littlewood in responding to the brief that culture should not be considered elitist.[10] Today cultural relativism is commonly accepted and, characteristic of New Labour, it has become the stuff of big business partnerships. Culture is widely thought to be an instrument to encourage social inclusion, and architecture is thought to be an instrument to create 'sustainable communities'. Then attempts at inclusivity must have seemed a daring challenge to convention.

'We were young and it was very much an "in your face" kind of building,' says the established Piano of 2005. Pompidou was 'a double provocation: a challenge to academics but also a parody of the technological imagery of our time,' in which 'the brightly colored metal and tubing serves an urban, symbolic, and expressive function, not a technical one.'[11] In what serves perfectly as a criticism of the superficiality of Pompidou-derived 'high tech', or the fetish of structural Expressionism, the man credited by Banham with the idea of the megastructure, Fumihiko Maki, had more sensibly suggested in 1964 that 'our cities must change as social and economic use dictates, and yet they must not be "temporary" in the worst visual sense'.[12] Maki, in turn, credits Kenzo Tange with the early insight, although the *Japan Architect* quote is not referenced:

Short-lived items are becoming more and more short-lived, and the cycle of change is shrinking at a corresponding rate. On the other hand, the accumulation of capital has made it possible to build in large-scale operations. Reformations of natural topography, dams, harbors, and highways are of a size and scope that involve long cycles of time, and these are the man-made works that tend to divide the overall system of the age. The two tendencies – towards shorter cycles and towards longer cycles – are both necessary to modern life and to humanity itself.

Banham repeats the unreferenced quote in *Megastructure*,[13] but *Japan Architect* had no archive to search.[14] Nevertheless, the correction to Davey's question about mere bigness in a machine age was suggested by Fumihiko Maki in his *Investigations in Collective Form*, which considered the conscious process of urban design, and 'established three major approaches':
• Compositional Form – Compositional Approach
• Mega-Structure (Form) – Structural Approach
• Group-Form – Sequential Approach

'The first of these, the compositional approach, is a historical one. The second two are new, and are efforts towards finding master forms that satisfy the demands of contemporary urban growth and change.'[15]

Kisho Kurokawa, proposal for the Pompidou Centre, Paris, 1971
The large floor-grids are arranged as an extendable 'urban hill', with roof gardens, and a 'sky escalator' from the water garden up to the restaurant level. The whole was intended to be highly lit up at night.

Kisho Kurokawa in his studio in 1970.

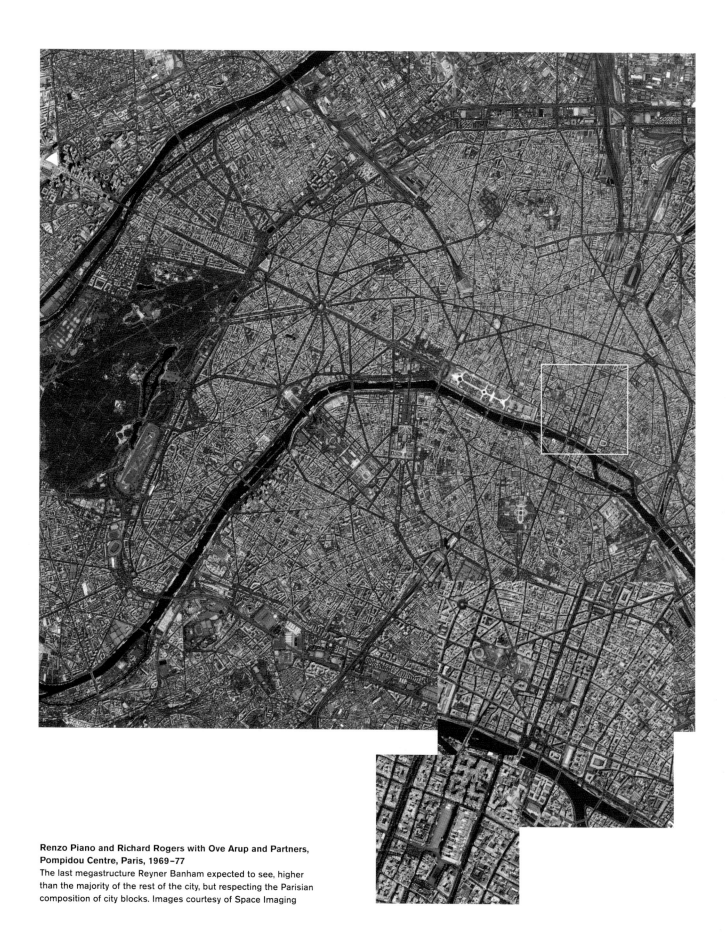

Renzo Piano and Richard Rogers with Ove Arup and Partners, Pompidou Centre, Paris, 1969–77
The last megastructure Reyner Banham expected to see, higher than the majority of the rest of the city, but respecting the Parisian composition of city blocks. Images courtesy of Space Imaging

Fumihiko Maki had more sensibly suggested in 1964 that 'our cities must change as social and economic use dictates, and yet they must not be "temporary" in the worst visual sense'.

For Maki, the compositional approach was the conventional way in which large-scale urban design is carried out, as an extension of the architectural approach of making a building out of components. Composition was about how different buildings created urban space. Banham also shows that the importance of composition in architecture was inherited by 20th-century Modernists, who imagined they had departed from the traditions of the academies modelled on the École des Beaux-Arts in Paris from the 19th century.[16] Composition is the approach that architects prefer and, consequently, as Martin Pawley put it in *Theory and Design in the Second Machine Age*, manufacturing outstrips construction, so that 'with or without regard to the pace at which "artists" can assimilate it, global product distribution is overwhelming the construction industry, and with it the architectural profession.'[17]

In contrast, the sequential approach, which drew inspiration from medieval cities in Europe, towns on Greek Islands or villages in northern Africa, aimed to generate an urban form by the repetitive use of a typical building unit. Over 40 years ago, Maki had provided an elegant way of expressing a development strategy based on variations on a theme of repetitive types, which in the past would have been built with local crafts and materials, but today could be manufactured internationally. Our interest in 'megastructures' for this issue of Δ led back to Maki,[18] with the added benefit of the sequencing approach of 'group form', in contrast to 'composition', and thanks to Reyner Banham and Jennifer Taylor. Given the denial of freehold in the UK,[19] a typological approach to planning has interested us at www.audacity.org for some time.[20]

Of course, in practice all three approaches – compositional, megastructural and typologically sequential – are mixed and matched, and carried out at varying densities of development. Maki insists that these are not antagonistic patterns, but can coexist in one configuration.[21] It is easy to miss this point, since Kenzo Tange's well-published Tokyo Bay proposal of 1960, the masterpiece in Banham's view, was so stridently megastructural. Tange had 'raised the scale of the megastructure argument to a level of monumental vastness from which it could not get down again'.[22] Also, Maki's

'structural approach' might be equally applied to development dispersed through an infrastructural landscape, to megastructures isolated in the landscape, such as Kisho Kurokawa's agricultural city,[23] or to big shed architecture in the suburbs.

However, in the UK there is at present little chance of experimenting with Maki's megastructural or sequential approaches on any substantial scale at any density, despite the legacy of British architects and engineers considered collectively as 'high tech'.[24] British architects have long been in the business of showing the structure and servicing of their buildings, but never got further than a few exemplars. Their history dips in and out of the construction industry effort around the sophistication and integration of building services.[25] Through the Lloyds Building, which took eight years to finish in 1986, Rogers did retain a sense of the architectural tension between built quality and social impermanence. So in his *Architecture: A Modern View of 1990*:

Present day concern for single objects will be replaced by concern for relationships. Shelters will no longer be static objects, but dynamic frameworks. Accommodation will be responsive, ever-changing and ever-adjusting. Cities of the future will no longer be zoned as today in isolated one-activity ghettos; rather, they will resemble the more richly layered cities of the past. Living, work, shopping, learning and leisure will overlap and be housed in continuous, varied and changing structures.[26]

Written at a poignant moment in history, Rogers expected a social dividend from the end of the Cold War and a 'new age of enlightenment' for capitalism to prioritise international poverty alleviation and the environment. Fifteen years later he continues to tune his theory of architectural expression in terms of 'legibility' and flexibility'. The idea that 'work, leisure and domestic activities are becoming interchangeable, leading to the creation of open-ended, flexible structures,' sounds similar to Maki, but Rogers means to resist development unless it is part of the compact city, regardless of whether a suburban house might equally accommodate his blurring of

Levitt & Sons, Levittown, New York, late 1940s/early 1950s
This is clearly a low-density sequential approach. Although
popular as built and adapted over time, done again today
the sequence and types would be more sophisticated.
Images courtesy of Space Imaging

the working day into the imagined 'fun' of housework. The requirement that 'these buildings, with their legible facades and logical form, relate directly to both the user and passers-by,' sounds engaging, but prioritises aesthetic clarity and order over the practical process of periodic refitting of the building around the changing and interrelated demands of the occupants. The Lloyds Building only looks flexible. Stockbrokers are not busy adapting it.

Rogers clearly feels the need for people to engage with his design in the same way as New Labour is desperate to consult on every policy, hoping to involve 'all the key stakeholders of a project'.[27] Yet he qualifies this by insisting on '"natural" means of achieving benign environmental conditions ... working with the climate, rather than trying to defeat it'.[28] The flexibility to upgrade the fabric and design in efficient

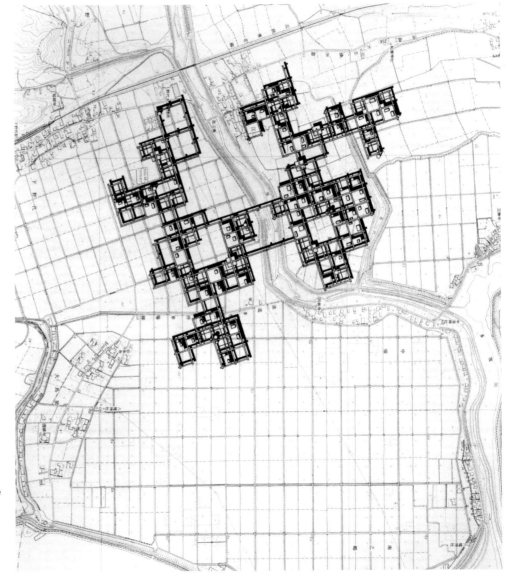

Kisho Kurokawa, Agricultural City, 1960
Intended for the replacement of the agricultural towns in Aichi destroyed by a typhoon in 1959, the accommodation was to be raised above the ground to deal with future flooding. The grid was intended to be between 300 and 500 metres (980 and 1640 feet), and Kurokawa challenged the assumption that the city and the country need be in antagonism.

air-conditioning is the wrong request. Just as all the consultation around the Urban Task Force report *Towards an Urban Renaissance*[29] presupposed urban development, making it pointless for most people asked the question 'Where do you want to live?' to answer with 'In a big house with a garden, please'.

The obsession with urban compaction is not just a brake on building at low density. It encourages a 'small is beautiful' mindset. Even Renzo Piano, trying to add to the composition of London by building beautifully up to 305 metres (1016 feet),[30] has faced massive opposition and delay.[31] Clusters of towers are finally coming through in the City of London and downriver at Canary Wharf in the old docklands, but all lower than the 324-metre (1080-foot) Eiffel Tower, built for the International Exhibition of Paris of 1889.[32] Getting over the fifth-of-a-mile-high barrier is proving difficult. Critics like Hugh Pearman weakly support skyscrapers, arguing that 'when you gaze across the green fields of Albion a few years hence and see them marking the cities on the horizon, consider this: if it wasn't for them, maybe those green fields wouldn't be there at all'.[33] To which many say: 'Yes, but we don't want those towers either!' Pearman never takes up the argument about scale and dynamic, but reinforces the grossly false impression that the UK is too small to allow development in the countryside, supposed to be dwindling away.

So we are reduced to crouching and cramming. All Yvette Cooper, Minister for Housing and Planning, could boast at the Royal Town Planning Institute in June 2005, was that 'the national average for density is now at 39 dwellings per hectare, up from only 25 in 1997, thanks to the Density Direction. 67% of new dwellings are being built on brownfield land compared to 57% in 1997.'[34]

The 2005 upgrade of the Richard Rogers Partnership website is worth reading. RRP insists that 'compact polycentric cities are the only sustainable form of development and should be designed to attract people. If we don't get urban regeneration right then all our work on cities – buildings and public spaces, education, health, employment, social inclusion and economic growth – will be undermined.'[35]

This is Little Britain, which imagines it is a small country,[36] devoted to participatory democracy on a small planet threatened by (American and Asian) industrialists.[37] We will not risk allowing ourselves adaptable living space by expanding cities upwards or outwards. The only thing the British do promptly on a massive scale is object to development, unless all participants can be assured at planning that the architectural composition will stabilise the economy, lead to social harmony and save the environment. No serious enterprise can truthfully manage that.

Consequently, the planning process in Little Britain is more about mendacity than audacity, and not at all about manufacturing modular architecture as a megastructure or a sequence of types. ⌂

Notes

1. Peter Davey, comment, 'Bigness', *Architectural Review*, August 2002, pp 4–5.
2. Reyner Banham, *Theory and Design in the First Machine Age*, Architectural Press (Oxford), 1997, first published 1960.
3. Dennis Sharp, 'Kenzo Tange (1913–2005)', *Architectural Review*, May 2005, p 36.
4. www.kikutake.co.jp, accessed 26 June 2005.
5. www.kisho.co.jp, accessed 26 June 2005.
6. Reyner Banham, *Megastructure: Urban Futures of the Recent Past*, Thames and Hudson (London), 1976, p 9.
7. Clough Williams-Ellis, *England and the Octopus*, Geoffrey Bles (London), 1928, facsimile edition (London, Council for the Protection of Rural England, 1996).
8. David Jeremiah, *Architecture and Design for the Family in Britain: 1900–1970*, Manchester University Press, 2000.
9. Kiyonori Kikutake, 'The great Shrine of Izumo', *World Architecture*, number 2, 1965, p 13.
10. Philip Jodidio, *Piano: Renzo Piano Building Workshop 1966–2005*, Taschen (London), 2005, p 7.
11. Renzo Piano quoted in Philip Jodidio, op cit, p 43.
12. Fumihiko Maki, *Investigations in Collective Form*, Washington University School of Architecture (St Louis, MO), 1964, p 4. http://library.wustl.edu/ units/spec/archives/photos/maki/m aki-entire.pdf, accessed 24 July 2005.
13. Reyner Banham, *Megastructure*, op cit, p 217.
14. www.japan-architect.co.jp, accessed 27 July 2005.
15. Maki, op cit, pp 5–6.
16. Reyner Banham, *Theory and Design in the First Machine Age*, op cit, pp 14–22.
17. Martin Pawley, *Theory and Design in the Second Machine Age*, Basil Blackwell (Oxford), 1990, p 10.
18. www.maki-and-associates.co.jp, accessed 24 July 2005.
19. Ian Abley, 'Development rights for the hydrogen-fuelled future', in Ian Abley and James Heartfield (eds), *Sustaining Architecture in the Anti-Machine Age*, Wiley-Academy (Chichester), 2001, pp 210–27.
20. James Woudhuysen and Ian Abley, *Why is Construction So Backward?*, Wiley-Academy (Chichester), 2004, p 287.
21. Maki and Associates, Gary Kamemoto, Mark Mulligan, Tohru Onuma, and Geoffrey Moussas (eds), *Fumihiko Maki: Buildings and Projects*, Thames and Hudson (London), 1997, p 206.
22. Reyner Banham, *Megastructure*, op cit, p 57.
23. Maki, op cit, p 14.
24. James S Russell, 'Introduction', *Pioneering British 'High-Tech'*, Phaidon (London), 1999, part of the '3 Architectures' series that reprinted titles from the 'Architecture in Detail' series: John McKean, *James Stirling and James Gowan – Leicester University Engineering Building 1959–63*, Phaidon (London), 1994; Gabriele Bramante, *Foster Associates – Willis Faber & Dumas Building Ipswich 1975*, Phaidon (London), 1993; Kenneth Powell, *Richard Rogers Partnership – Lloyds Building 1978–86*, Phaidon (London), 1994.
25. Reyner Banham, *The Architecture of the Well-Tempered Environment*, University of Chicago Press, 1984, 2nd edn, first published 1969.
26. Richard Rogers, *Architecture: A Modern View*, Thames and Hudson (London), 1990, p 60.
27. www.richardrogers.co.uk, accessed 4 May 2005.
28. Richard Rogers, 'Towards Sustainable Architecture – Environmental Research and Development at RRP', www.richardrogers.co.uk, accessed 4 May 2005.
29. Urban Task Force, *Towards an Urban Renaissance: Final Report of the Urban Task Force*, DETR, E&FN Spon (London), 1999.
30. Jodidio, op cit, pp 489–93.
31. www.londonbridgetower.com , accessed 3 August 2005.
32. www.tour-eiffel.fr/teiffel/uk/, accessed 3 August 2005.
33. Hugh Pearman, 'The only way is up: high-rise hits Britain, and this time they mean it', *Gabion*, 2004. www.hughpearman.com/ articles5/skyscrapers4.html, accessed 3 August 2005.
34. Yvette Cooper MP, Minister for Housing and Planning, speech to the Royal Town Planning Institute Annual Planning Convention, 30 June 2005, www.odpm.gov.uk, accessed 30 July 2005.
35. www.richardrogers.co.uk, accessed 3 May 2005.
36. Richard Rogers and Anne Power, *Cities for a Small Country*, Faber (London), 2000.
37. Richard Rogers, *Cities for a Small Planet*, Faber (London), 1997.

Fumihiko Maki

The Japanese Pritzker Prize winning
architect Fumihiko Maki is credited with
coining the term 'megastructure'. Here,
Jennifer Taylor describes how he has
refined it, and defined a specific way of
handling urban megacompositions that
he calls 'group form', over the course of a
career spanning more than four decades.

The thinking of Fumihiko Maki was
seminal to the radical avant-garde of
the 1960s, which turned to the notions
of technology and Futuristic structures
of great size to cope with the urban
problems facing the cities of Europe
and Japan. Maki was chosen as the 1993
Laureate of the Pritzker Architecture
Prize,[1] and his concepts are the basis
of much urban thinking today.

Maki's urban theories need to be
positioned alongside the state of mind
in the profession in the 1960s, when
Team X's structuralist theories were
propounded by the radical avant-garde
of Europe. Further, Maki's early work
has to be seen in the context of Japan
in the postwar era when the search for
answers to the Japanese urban crisis
was real and pressing. He first became
well known as one of the Metabolists, a
radical group of Japanese architects who
proposed many visionary solutions.
His concepts on adaptive planning were
given public voice in his contribution,
with Masato Ohtaka, to the Metabolist

Group's publication *Metabolism:
Proposals for New Urbanism*, released in
1960.[2] The writings and schemes of the
Metabolists were primarily concerned
with new forms of urban order that
would accept the conditions of a nuclear
world and lead to the revitalisation of
the Japanese city. While these Futuristic
proposals relied on advanced
technologies, the concepts were
basically organic, as the city would be
continually regenerated by continuous
replacement of parts on a 'metabolic
cycle', as in nature.

The ideas of Metabolism were
elaborated on by Maki in his writing of
1964, *Investigations in Collective Form*,[3]
where he identifies three possibilities
for accommodating the superhuman
scale of modern systems and units
by systems of 'collective form':
conventional 'composition',
'megastructure' and 'group form'. These
ideas have been expanded upon in *Japan
Architect*,[4] and his practice profile,
with Maki concluding that 'group form'

was the most appropriate strategy
for the handling of megaprojects in a
dynamic, open-ended way.[5]

While Maki was involved in exploring
the megastructure in the design studios
at Harvard, and is credited as the first to
use the term, he rejects it in favour of
'group form'. In this approach, a project
is designed in such a way that the
overall governing structure is evident,
and brings cohesion, while the parts
that lead to the whole are related in a
state of 'dynamic equilibrium', open to
addition and subtraction.

These theories were first applied in
an exploratory project for the Shinjuku
Station Development, Tokyo, in 1960. At
Hillside Terraces, Tokyo, from 1969 Maki
designed a sequence of residential
additions over several decades, with the
development dynamically growing and
evolving through time.[6] The same design
principles underlie the megaprojects of
the 1980s and 1990s, such as the Tokyo
Metropolitan Gymnasium (1990), treated
as a cluster of diverse, yet related,

Maki Associates, Republic Polytechnic, Singapore, 2005
The buildings of this 'group form' complex are located on the basis of function and desirable accessibility with a central nucleus 'Learning Hub' and satellite supporting facilities, all linked by bridges and covered walkways. The Learning Hub consists of 11 identical pods and one administration unit supporting two central elliptical open terraces that provide connections, and recreational and specialised teaching units.

Maki Associates, Tokyo Metropolitan Gymnasium, 1990
This inner-city sports centre is typical of Maki's large-span megaprojects, with the bulk of the complex broken down into individual parts – the main arena, small arena, swimming pool and ancillary structures – all related in an open-ended composition.

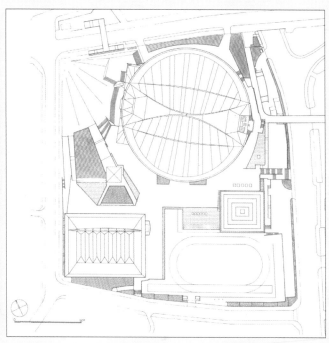

buildings united, but remaining open to change. The Republic Polytechnic, Singapore (2005), with its uniting suspended platforms that tie the central elements together, provides an exemplar of Maki's intentions in planning such architectural projects as receptive, open, yet engaged interventions.

Since the early thinking of the 1960s, in Maki's work the megaproject has been treated as a collective form of many parts. This approach allows for an overriding cohesive 'bigness' based on a policy of accepting and accommodating the large, through strategies of grouping, incompleteness and the rejection of closure.[7] △

Notes
1. www.pritzkerprize.com/maki2.htm, accessed 1 September 2005.
2. K Kikutake, N Kawazoe, M Ohtaka, F Maki, and N Kurokawa, *Metabolism: The Proposals for New Urbanism*, Yasuko Kawazoe (Tokyo), 1960.
3. Fumihiko Maki, with Masato Ohtaka and Jerry Goldberg, *Investigations in Collective Form*, Washington University School of Architecture (St Louis, MO), 1964.
4. Fumihiko Maki, 'Notes on Collective Form', *Japan Architect*, winter 1994, pp 247–97.
5. Maki and Associates, Gary Kamemoto, Mark Mulligan, Tohru Onuma and Geoffrey Moussas (eds), *Fumihiko Maki: Buildings and Projects*, Princeton Architectural Press (New York), 1997, pp 206–17.
6. www.hillsideterrace.com/english/history-story.html, accessed 3 August 2005.
7. Jennifer Taylor, *The Architecture of Fumihiko Maki: Space, City, Order and Making*, Birkhauser (Basel), 2003.

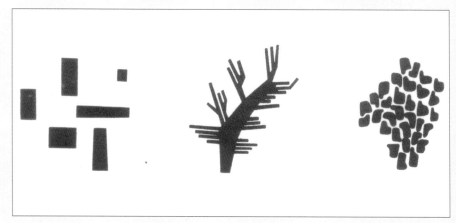

Approaches to collective form: compositional form, megaform and group form respectively.

People, Not Architecture, Make Communities

Community is an illusive and, in many respects, unpredictable quality. A sense of citizenship does not simply follow on from a replication of the Victorian, walkable city, just as public disengagement and a lack of social cohesion are not immediate attributes of car-based and low-density conurbations. As David Miliband MP, Minister of Communities and Local Government, asserts: 'Architecture on its own can't make communities.' Here, in conversation with James Heartfield, Miliband discusses the problems at the heart of sustainable communities – at a time of pending urgency as housing demand far outstrips supply.

The supply of new homes is out of balance with demand, says David Miliband, and we need to build many more houses. This is a challenge that has dogged his boss, Deputy Prime Minister John Prescott, whose demand for a 'step-change' in the building of new homes did not substantially redress the balance.

Part of Miliband's difficulty is the extreme reaction to the proposal to build new homes, especially in the Thames Gateway. According to historian Tristram Hunt, the development is a 'tsunami of concrete' to accommodate 'London's monstrous growth', 'year-zero vandalism dressed up as regeneration,'[1] and the 'massive construction programme set to engulf what remains of the UK's rural heritage.'[2] The Campaign to Protect Rural England (CPRE) warns that, by 2035, the countryside as we know it will cease to exist.[3] Pointing out that just 11 per cent of England is built up has little impact on the deep-seated prejudice that we are concreting over the countryside.

Miliband is listening to people's anxieties over new building, but he checks them by saying that 'there is an anxiety among parents that their children will not have somewhere to live'. The shortfall is due to increased demand, as the number of families increases, while the supply of new homes has slumped to a level that cannot replace the old, worn-out stock.

Over and above the fear of urbanisation, building projects have provoked anxieties that the new residential areas will not be real, or 'sustainable', communities. Confronted by the objections of Conservative MPs, Miliband accused them of 'denouncing plans for new building as the end of civilisation as we know it'.[4] This is important given that the anxieties voiced about the development of communities in the Thames Gateway come close to being an alibi for not building at all.

'There is no architectural magic wand for sustainable communities,' Miliband told me on the roof terrace at the Office of the Deputy Prime Minister (ODPM) in London's Victoria. 'Architecture on its own can't make a community.' This is a theme he has made his own. 'Civic pride depends on people, not structures,' he told the Core Cities Group on 20 May 2005.[5]

Civic pride cannot be designed into the Thames Gateway. It can only be created by the people who already live there, or will come to live there. Hunt's belief that 'an injection of local, vernacular architecture' will provide 'individual homes and towns with a sense of connection with the past' is not just tawdry nostalgia, a willingness to invent a past that never was, but a false belief that buildings make communities.

As Miliband argues: 'It is people, not houses, who make communities.'

'Community is about identity, but also about agency – about the ability to act,' he says.

Anxiety about a lack of community in the new developments is profound, echoing the anxieties about 'soulless suburbia' that have troubled the moaning classes for more than a century. At its heart is a sense of alienation from the mass of ordinary people. This is the barely concealed subtext to anti-development arguments.

'New homes spread like so much detritus discarded across thousands of hectares of southern England. Plots of land the size of handkerchiefs, crumpled into the nowhere lands of the Thames Gateway, the M11 corridor and greater Milton Keynes. Hundreds of thousands of new homes: red-tiled, UPVC windowed, developers' junk.'

Architectural critic Jonathan Glancey, imagining the year 2020, gave vent to his hatred of suburbia, and the nowhere people of the ODPM-identified 'growth areas'. He goes on:

James Heartfield interviews David Miliband, MP for South Shields and Minister of Communities and Local Government, in September 2005.

'This is what most of us fear when we think of future housing. An England made more subtopian than suburban ... Ever more cul-de-sac estates linked together by raging arterial roads lined with chain stores ... Superstores. Multiplexes. Distribution depots. An England 100% England Free. A getting-and-spending logoed and baseball-capped land chock full of call centres and staffed by customer service facility managers.'[6]

Presumably Glancey would say similar things about ideas for megastructures, or system-built towers at Thamesmead, because this is not really about the architecture. What appears to be a discussion of housing turns out to be an expression of revulsion at the masses, characterised here by their consumer lifestyles, or at least those imagined for them by Glancey. But these are only 'nowhere lands' for those to whom the people who live in them appear alien and, by dint of that, an undifferentiated mass, less people than a 'tsunami of concrete'. 'In the halcyon days of the postwar welfare state,' says Miliband, the foundation of social-democratic power was 'a relatively homogeneous working-class base', but that 'has now been shattered'.[7]

The disaggregation of the working-class base of social democracy is the condition that reduces the people to a mass in the eyes of intellectuals like Hunt and Glancey.

Of course, working-class communities are only ever romanticised when they are fading from sight. In their lauded book *Family and Kinship in East London*, Peter Wilmot and Michael Young divined a 'sense of belonging' that was 'so deep because it is rooted in a lasting attachment to their families'.[8] But these same East London communities were despised by middle-class radicals before they were cleared to make way for new buildings. Their 'rookeries' were seen as hotbeds of crime and depravity; the weavers' own independent schools in Spitalfields were so threatening that the government agreed to fund church schools to undermine them.

The very idea of community is loaded with all kinds of presuppositions. It is unlikely that any contemporary community would be geographically based. People are much more likely to organise on the basis of common activities, whether cultural or through work. But, above all, communities are rarely ever built from the top down. The desire to build community into new housing developments indicates nervousness on the part of those in charge that people will gather in unexpected and even unwelcome ways if they are not carefully guided.

In the Thames Gateway, people will create the communities that are appropriate to them. In today's conditions they are likely to be ad hoc and even fleeting. But they will not organise themselves conveniently into the provided community centres or neighbourhood-watch groups, and any communities will be made of human beings, not architecture and construction.

On 30 June 2004 a barge, organised by the Department for Culture, Media and Sport, leaves the Savoy Pier near Westminster Bridge. On board are Lord Rogers of Riverside, assorted developers, journalists, including the design critic Stephen Bayley, Mark Brearley of the Greater London Authority, and me. We are going down the Thames, to Thurrock, epicentre of the Thames Gateway development, to hear the Culture Secretary, Tessa Jowell, tell us that in Thurrock 'culture is at the heart of regeneration'. The priority of the arts over development is emphasised by Housing Minister Keith Hill's apologies for not being able to make it.

Also absent are the people of Thurrock, whose future some 300 dignitaries have assembled in the Tilbury Cruise Terminal to discuss. 'One hardly knew such places existed,'

Richard Rogers at the Tilbury Cruise Terminal, Thurrock, where he presented his vision for the Thames Gateway to an audience invited by the Department for Culture, Media and Sport, 30 June 2004.

says a bemused Bayley. Our little boat flew the pennant of Tate (never 'the Tate') courtesy of gallery director Nicholas Serota, reinforcing the impression that we have come to civilise the natives.

Tessa Jowell is emphatic that 'we want to avoid the pitfalls of regeneration', such as 'the Hoxton effect, where regeneration becomes gentrification'. She is full of ideas about heritage: 'As we can see with the Baltic Exchange in Newcastle, the reuse of historic buildings has a positive effect for regeneration.' In her speech, she emphasises the common ground between the Deputy Prime Minister and the Chairman of the Urban Task Force, the architect Richard Rogers: 'As John Prescott has said, there is no urban renaissance without good design.'

In his presentation, Rogers gives a nod towards design, before plunging into some alarming mathematics designed to show that 304,000 households could be crammed into the 38,000 hectares of derelict land running along 43 miles of the Thames at 80 homes to the hectare. Of course he has his sums wrong: at that density, 38,000 hectares would house 3 million households, not 300,000. And in any case, the Thames Gateway totals some 80,000 hectares, with 600,000 households already living there. Yet the ODPM was only initially planning 120,000 additional homes in total by 2016. As its annual report makes clear, that figure is, in fact, an addition of only 40,000 to older planning targets.[9] But none of these facts mattered to the audience. Rogers could pose as challenging the official figure, when in reality he was out by a factor of 10 on his own logic.

If, as is suggested by the editors of this magazine, a Thames Gateway of 3 million households were to be built over 25 years, 96,000 homes per year are required to add 2.4 million to the 600,000 already there, assuming the existing didn't need replanning – which is likely. That would be like building another London to the east of the existing one, and would no doubt mean a lot of additional rebuilding of existing development. Nor would it all need to be a monotone 80 homes a hectare. Even without building on, say, 25 per cent of the 'growth area' – because there are great places through the estuary landscape worth keeping and a need for new landscapes – the 60,000 hectares could easily accommodate 3 million households with all the activities, services and infrastructure that such a population requires. The density of development might range from less than one-home-a-hectare smallholdings to many thousands-of-homes-a-hectare mile-high towers.

Yet none of this ambition is on offer. Rogers has recently echoed architect Terry Farrell, who oddly proposes building on very little of the Thames Gateway at the London end, valuing the existing pylon-riddled emptiness well beyond the merit of all but the most exceptional estuary landscape and wildlife.[10] This basically says don't build on the Thames Gateway, or anything other than a clump of architect-designed compact city. But then that is the Urban Task Force's agenda: if there must be more homes stack them high, to keep the countryside pristine. Pile them up in a few bits of the Thames Gateway, such as 'Stratford City' or 'City East', if they must be built at all,[11] in an attempt to design community into the 'sustainable' architecture.[12]

Try again … 38,000 x 80 = 3,040,000 households.

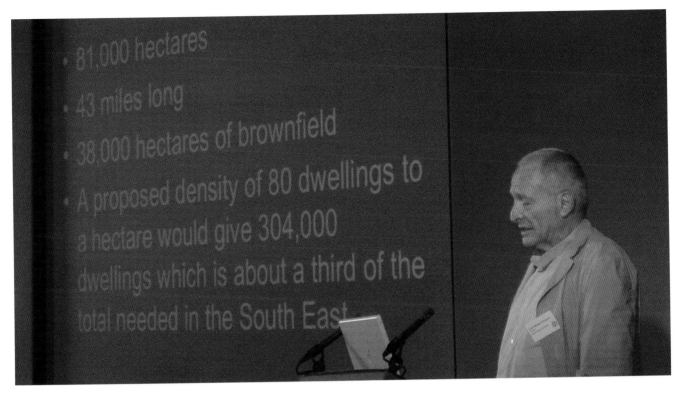

Did Rogers' dodgy maths reveal a subconscious fixation with the numbers? Perhaps! In any case, back at Thurrock, he need hardly have bothered. The underlying message of the day seemed to be that there is no intention to house 700,000 people in 304,000 homes.[13] The 'Visionary Brief in the Thames Gateway' is being dissipated fast, as the event begins to look like a workshop on sustainable living at the World Social Forum. The Dutch artist Jeanne van Heewijk is reporting back from her 'one-day charette' – 'an intensive, multidisciplinary brainstorming workshop where visionary ideas are encouraged' – with 'spectacularist' Keith Khan. They think that development must take place over an 11-year time cycle, and that before there is any volume building, 'ten innovative prototype houses' should be made by teams of one architect, one potential resident, one artist and one ecologist. No, this is not a 'how many to change a light bulb' joke.

Instead of dismissing this proposal for the impractical, time-wasting job-creation scheme that it is, the Culture Secretary said it was 'inspiring' – and endorsed it. Three-hundred-and-four thousand people housed? At this rate you would be lucky to have 10 custom-built, eco-friendly wigwams sinking into the mudflats in 11 years. As the charettes reported back, the phrase 'volume building' was used as a swear word, the negative of 'environment', 'culture' or 'design'.

But as David Miliband says: 'If, by "volume", is meant large numbers of different kinds of architecture, that is what people want.' In the audience at Thurrock, though, the established volume house-builders shrank back into their seats, the uncultured villains of the piece, gloomily calculating the costs of subcontracting the design to an ecologist, an artist, an architect and a resident to be, factoring in an 11-year wait, before concluding that they could do better business elsewhere. ⚏

Notes
1. Tristram Hunt, 'Grow with the Flow', *The Guardian*, Comment, 26 July 2005. www.guardian.co.uk/comment/story/0,,1536013,00.html, accessed 26 July 2005.
2. Tristram Hunt, 'Labour betrays heritage, and its history', *The Observer*, Comment, 8 December 2002. http://observer.guardian.co.uk/politics/story/0,,856246,00.html, accessed 26 July 2005.
3. Paul Kingsnorth, *Your Countryside, Your Choice*, Campaign to Protect Rural England, 2005. www.cpre.org.uk, accessed 20 September 2005.
4. David Miliband, 'Civic pride for the modern age', speech to the Core Cities Group, 20 May 2005. www.odpm.gov.uk, accessed 10 June 2005.
5. www.corecities.com, accessed 4 August 2005.
6. Jonathan Glancey, 'Home Truths', 'The World in 2020' supplement, *The Guardian*, 25 September 2004, p 10. www.guardian.co.uk/2020/story/0,,1309403,00.html, accessed 26 July 2005.
7. David Miliband, 'New Labour in power again – what next?', lecture at the Friedrich-Ebert-Stiftung, Berlin, 21 February 2002. www.feslondon.dial.pipex.com/ pubs02/milib-3e.htm, accessed 10 June 2005.
8. Peter Wilmot and Michael Young, *Family and Kinship in East London*, Penguin (Harmondsworth), 1980, first published 1957, p 187.
9. ODPM *Annual Report 2004*, 4 May 2004, p 8. www.odpm.gov.uk, accessed 2 June 2004.
10. Terry Farrell and Partners, 'Landscape – The First Infrastructure', emailed to guest-editor Ian Abley, 1 March 2004.
11. Vikki Miller, 'Rogers' taskforce calls for communities plan to be axed', *Building*, 16 September 2005, p 11.
12. Ellen Bennett, 'Rogers in bid to halt white flight', *Building Design*, 16 September 2005, p 1.
13. Vikki Miller, 'Prescott to bring Rogers back into centre of policy debate', *Building*, 8 July 2005, p 13.

London 2030
Taking the Thames Gateway Seriously

Encouraged by Will Alsop's Supercities project, **Ian Abley** produced this map as an open invitation to start imagining the development of the Thames Gateway – a doubling of London to the east. Your proposals and visions for a rethought London can be sent through to the guest-editor of this issue of *D* at www.audacity.org.

What if the Thames Gateway were all done at once and in quick time to pay for the transportation, services and infrastructure needed to double London?

The allocated growth area is about 80,000 hectares (200,000 acres). That is, seven times bigger than the total of real estate owned, operated and upgraded on a daily basis by Wal-Mart, as discussed by the Box Tank later in this issue. One equivalent of Wal-Mart is 11,660 hectares (28,810 acres), 117 square kilometres (45 square miles), or the blue square shown here approximately to scale with sides of 10.79 kilometres (6.71 miles). At 39 households per hectare, the current British average, the Wal-Mart estate amounts to 299,000 dwellings, or 1.75 years at the current rate of British annual house production.

Yet to double Greater London from 7 to 14 million inhabitants, we only need to develop 75 per cent of the whole gateway, at the full range of densities, as compositions, megastructures and sequences, and using as many methods of

construction as can deliver a megacity. That is a mere five Wal-Marts – or 1 Wal-Mart equivalent every five years to 2030.

Such a scale of thinking could connect the estuary to central London with an enlarged road network and all sorts of transit systems, including a magnetic levitation train. It could link north Kent to South Essex and provide the flood defences that the whole region needs, with new routes criss-crossing the Thames between new focal points of mile-high megastructures.

Whether by tunnel to a new airport, as Bluebase anticipate, or over an inhabited bridge between Thamesmead and Dagenham, as Will Alsop envisages, there must be more to the Thames Gateway than a few microflats stacked up to six storeys on the scraps of brownfield land that are trickling out of the complex of regeneration agencies.

'Modernise our Homes' sounds like the plea of the local community, and maybe for those who want to stay in Thamesmead, or can't get out, it is. It is, in fact, a section of the banner produced by Gallions Housing Association, owner of Thamesmead, which reads 'Working in Partnership to Modernise our Homes'.

If there is one lesson to be learned from Thamesmead, with its systems, circulation and the medical centre on stilts over the 'lake', it is that fashionable architecture is never enough to sustain anything through periods of social change. What is needed is a political and economic dynamic that goes beyond the act of ventriloquism of policy-makers and developers talking through 'the community'.

After the east-coast floods of 1953, and completed in 1984 only to protect the old City of London, the beautiful Thames Barrier needs to be replaced by something bigger and better across the estuary that serves not only as a flood defence, but as a tidal power source and transport hub to a mile-high city cluster. Such a megastructural approach, solving a number of developmental problems by creating a number of developmental opportunities, and not least a magnetic levitation train route to what is presently central London, is sadly far from any official 'vision' for the Thames Estuary 'growth area'.

Clockwise, from top left: A sense of distance to low-rise London from Shooters Hill; the Dartford crossing of the bridge north to south, and the tunnel the other way, need to be relieved by several new crossings to tie the Thames Gateway together into a working region; the Old Ford site might be connected to Thamesmead as a reinvigorated site of architectural manufacturing, where the modules that the Thames Gateway are to be made from are produced, and linked with the international market through London's growing container facilities. The manufactured architecture will need to be bigger than shipping containers, but the same sorts of logistics apply.

All photographs courtesy of Simon Punter Photography, and part of a larger photographic survey of the Thames Gateway undertaken with www.audacity.org, to be published in 2006.

Megastructure as an inhabited single-storey participatory architectural production line over the Thames, August 2005, courtesy of Will Alsop with Tim Thornton.

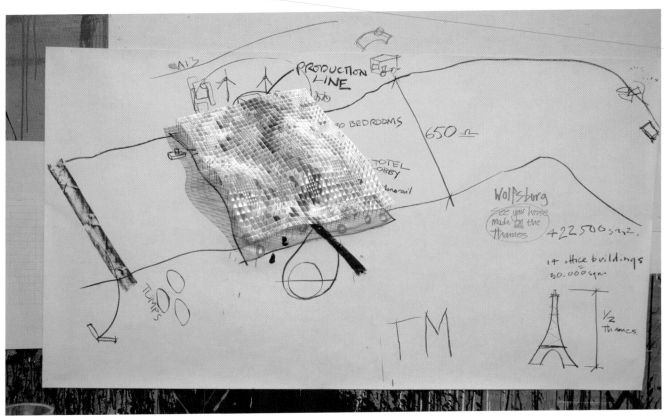

This square of the Thames Gateway serves as a perfect design-competition site for a modular megastructure over the Thames. The site is bounded by the A13, Ford and the Barking power station to the north, Rainham Marsh to the east, Thamesmead to the south and the sewage treatment works to the west. The image was taken before the Centre for Engineering and Manufacturing Excellence was complete. In 2006, www.audacity.org aims to arrange a design competition, and looks forward to Will Alsop's continuing kind support. Image courtesy of Space Imaging

Thames Reach Tunnel is an independent private-sector initiative to develop a high-capacity road, rail and utility connection under the Thames Sea Reach between Canvey Island in Essex and the Hoo Peninsula in Kent. The new multimodal tunnel connections transform the historic, radial infrastructure of London north and south of the Thames into an orbital and circulatory system, enabling the Thames Gateway region to become an area of high growth. This is linked to a high-capacity, 24-hour airport serving the eastern hemisphere, integrated with London's next generation of sea defences, and provides new utility connections incorporating energy farms in the Thames Estuary. For further information see www.bluebase.com.

Travelling in a Straight Line

In the 1970s, when Paul Rudolph's Lower Manhattan Expressway project was featured on the cover of Reyner Banham's *Megastructure*, no urban scheme was complete without a rapid transit system running through it. Today, cities are serviced and connected by a range of technologies. Architect and technology-transfer enthusiast **Oliver Houchell** talks about the need to use these to increase mobility and expand capacity into and between the world's megalopoli.

Alongside tunnels, the most prevalent typology of manmade modular infrastructure today is the bridge. Unusually for an architectural practice, Wilkinson Eyre works on many forms of engineering structure,[1] and has been involved in bridge design since winning a competition to design the South Quay Bridge at Canary Wharf, London, which was completed in 1997.[2] The Gateshead Millennium Bridge, a pedestrian bridge that spectacularly pivots to allow shipping along the river Tyne, was also won in competition that year,[3] and completed in 2001.[4] The latest project, the Viaduc de la Savoureuse, is, at the time of writing, yet to be completed as part of the TGV (Train à Grande Vitesse) network.[5]

Part of the planned French Rhin–Rhône high-speed train link, the viaduct will cross the Savoureuse valley between Montbéliard and Belfort, about 40 kilometres (25 miles) from the border with Switzerland. It is the only part of the future line for which a design competition was organised, due to its location. The scheme extends over 1.3 kilometres (0.8 miles) of line, comprising the 800-metre-long (2,625-foot-long) viaduct and a stretch of significant earthworks through the raised, west bank of the valley. The viaduct will be visible from Autoroute 36 and Route Nationale No. 437, the banks of the Haute Saône canal and the river Savoureuse. It will also be seen from the nearby villages of Bermont and Trévenans, so an aspiration for the project was for the structure to be as delicate as possible, placing a clearly legible and elegant form across the landscape of the valley.

The bridge has been designed with a simple, rhythmic quality suggestive of the transfer of forces. The structural demands made by the TGV, which travels at up to 350 kilometres (220 miles) per hour, are substantial: most significant is vertical acceleration (deflection); other key considerations include the longitudinal traction force imposed

Wilkinson Eyre Architects, Viaduc de la Savoureuse, France, 2005–
To travel in a straight line it is necessary to raise the infrastructure above the terrain for the majority of the track length and allow open access beneath, whether in countryside or through built-up areas.

during braking and the extremely tight track tolerance for lateral movement. The structure, in comparison to its length, is low. Thus one of the design challenges was to ensure that the depth of the spanning deck remained in proportion to the mass of the piers, and that the piers, when viewed obliquely across the valley, did not obscure the view behind.

The scheme comprises a linear series of steel 'tetrapod' piers set into the landscape on pads. Lateral girders span between the piers and support the transversely spanning deck to create a slender linear profile. Each prefabricated tetrapod is composed of two V-shaped supports that create an open form derived from simple geometry to ensure the constructional viability of the modules. They each consist of an upturned cone from which the surplus volume is purged and the 'V' profiles are conceptually 'cut'.

The piers support the viaduct and bear down on to tapered concrete pads, which are used to account for changes in the natural ground level across the valley, and again have their origin in elemental cone geometry. A conventionally oriented cone (with its point uppermost) has four scallops removed from its volume, each scallop described as the removal of part of a canted cylinder, to create four reciprocal 'elevations' to the tetrapod piers.

The depth of the deck was kept to a minimum – 3.5 metres (11.5 feet) – by having relatively short spans between tetrapod piers, each of approximately 42 metres (138 feet), a ratio that would normally result in the closing off of the view across the valley if conventional mass piers were used.

Finally, a cutting will be required through the wooded, western bank of the valley to accommodate the lie of the tracks. The impact of such significant earthworks will be minimised by a planted bridge that will span the tracks to re-establish the tree line along the valley.

The Viaduc de la Savoureuse is relatively small in scale in comparison with some, such as Foster and Partners' remarkable Millau viaduct, also in France. Each of its sections spans 350 metres (1150 feet) and its columns range in height from 75 metres (250 feet) to 235 metres (770 feet) – higher than the Eiffel Tower – with the masts rising a further 90 metres (295 feet) above the road deck.[6] Such projects undoubtedly express 'a fascination with the relationships between function, technology and aesthetics in a graceful structural form.'[7]

The demand for such civil structures is set to increase. Populations are not only growing, they are becoming more mobile, leading to a demand for faster, more efficient infrastructural links, whether within the city centre, between the city and the airport, or between cities. Yet the national rail system in the UK has been fraught with problems over the past 30 or so years, the result of continuous neglect and underinvestment. The same has applied to the London Underground, though in stark contrast to the majority of the ailing network, the Jubilee Line extension has proven that underground rail stations and interchanges can be spacious, light and efficient. Wilkinson Eyre was also involved with Stratford Market Depot, completed in 1996, and Stratford Regional Station, completed in 1999.[8]

The UK also has a number of inner-city tramlines, but they often compete for the existing road infrastructure and face a deregulated bus industry that is in direct competition with future schemes. This is difficult territory in which to effect serious change, as the Light Rail Transit Association understands only too well.[9]

At the most technologically advanced end of rail transport is 'maglev', an abbreviation of the phenomenon of magnetic levitation. The basic levitation principle is familiar: the

opposite poles of two magnets force one another apart, the force increasing as they are brought closer together. The idea was first proposed over a hundred years ago, but it took until 2003 for the first maglev train to operate commercially, in Shanghai, China. Companies in Germany and Japan are also developing maglev train technologies, each with subtle differences that result in distinct advantages and disadvantages.

In essence, both use noncontact (frictionless), nonwearing guidance and propulsion systems based on electromagnetic levitation (or suspension, as in the case of the German Transrapid system, a joint company of Siemens and ThyssenKrupp).[10] These enable speeds of up to 500 kilometres (310 miles) per hour. The systems are quieter, more cost-efficient, have lower specific energy consumption than traditional wheel-on-rail systems, and are virtually impossible to derail. A head-on collision is impossible as the propulsion system only operates in one direction at any one time. The trains run on a guide rail that incorporates linear electromagnetic motors, providing greater power where it is required, such as in areas around stations and on steeper gradients. On braking, the system turns into a generator, able to provide power to be fed back into the grid system that supplies it. The land consumption of maglev systems is again low.

If the brief for the Viaduc de la Savoureuse had been for a maglev route rather than wheel-on-rail TGV, the impact on its design would probably have been significant. Without the need for a flat bearing deck on which to lay the tracks or an acoustic barrier, the span would appear slight. As most of the power would be supplied by the guide rail rather than by the train itself, the mass, and therefore inertia, of the train would be markedly less, resulting in lower longitudinal traction forces being applied to the supporting structure. The maglev system does not impose point loads, enabling the viaduct to bear the load of a train across more of its structure, which would lessen the bulk to the pier elevations. All this would result in a structure that touched the earth in a lighter manner. Finally, with a slender clearance envelope compared to wheel-on-rail predecessors, even the cut through the western bank of woodland might be reduced.

At the most extreme end of maglev proposals is a scheme by Ernst Frankel, retired professor of ocean engineering at MIT, and Frank Davidson, a former MIT researcher and early member of the English Channel Tunnel study group. 'The idea is as wondrous as it is audacious,' says popular science writer Carl Hoffman in his column Conspicuous Construction. 'Get on a train at New York City's Penn Station and hit Paris, London or Brussels just an hour later.' The proposal is for a neutrally buoyant and straight tunnel submerged 45 to 90 metres (150 to 300 feet) beneath the surface of the Atlantic, and anchored to the sea floor, avoiding the high pressures of the deep ocean. The maglev trains would travel at an astounding 6440 kilometres (4000 miles) per hour through a vacuum within the tunnel enclosure to eliminate air friction and preclude the damaging effects on the tunnel of a sonic boom. Whilst the scientific principles behind the proposal appear sound, it seems likely that such an ambitious scheme may struggle to progress beyond the ideas stage. As Davidson said to Hoffman: 'A transatlantic tunnel will be done. We just have to be as interested in it as we are in getting to the Moon.'[11] That is precisely the problem.

Yet as populations increase we must improve our mobility, and increase travel speeds and efficiencies. In any form of movement, the greater the velocity the straighter the line of trajectory. Whether our journey is across the Thames Gateway, the UK, Europe or the world's oceans, to move fast we must travel in a straight line. ⚇

The tetrapod piers for the Viaduc de la Savoureuse.

Notes

1. Wilkinson Eyre Architects, Bridging Art and Science, Booth Clibborn Editions Ltd (London), 2001. www.booth-clibborn.com
2. Jeremy Melvin, Wilkinson Eyre – Bridges, Wilkinson Eyre Architects (London), 2003. www.wilkinsoneyre.com
3. Ian Abley and James Heartfield (eds), 'Beautifully simple', Sustaining Architecture in the Anti-Machine Age, Wiley-Academy (Chichester) 2001, pp 38–9.
4. www.gateshead.gov.uk/bridge/bridged.htm, accessed 30 July 2005.
5. www.tgv.co.uk, accessed 30 July 2005.
6. http://bridgepros.com/projects/Millau_Viaduct/, accessed 30 July 2005.
7. www.fosterandpartners.com/internetsite/html/Project.asp?JobNo=0778, accessed 30 July 2005.
8. Ian Abley and James Heartfield (eds), 'Lightness and Span' and 'The Well Tempered Environment', Sustaining Architecture in the Anti-Machine Age, Wiley-Academy (Chichester), 2001, pp 110–13.
9. www.lrta.org, accessed 30 July 2005.
10. www.transrapid.de, accessed 30 July 2005.
11. Carl Hoffman, 'Trans-Atlantic maglev – vacuum tube', Conspicuous Construction, April 2004. www.popsci.com/popsci/science/article/0,20967,781732,00.html, accessed 30 July 2005.

Cloud Piercer: Mile High

Conceived by **Jonathan Schwinge** as a hypothetical model for the tallest and largest megastructural project in world – the Thames Estuary – Cloud Piercer would be an oceanic vertical supercity to meet the rate of anticipated economic and population growth throughout the world.

Three 1610-metre (5280-foot), or 'mile high', steel lattice towers would be located north and west of Whitstable and Herne Bay in the Thames Estuary, south and east of Southend, off Sheppey. They are clear of the navigable channels along the Thames and into the Medway, and close to the Maunsell Sea Forts – an inspiration to Archigram we look at later in this issue in 'Architecture with Legs'. Standing within a 4610-metre (15,125-foot) diameter circular and inhabited wave breaker, which forms a protected harbour, the towers are surrounded by smaller, floating inhabited accommodation structures.

Each tower contains all the functions of a city, and provides a relief to, and extension of, overcrowded old London. The inhabitants of the three-tower cluster would have links to the mainland via ship, tiltrotor aircraft, coastal defence barrage and a submerged tunnel.

Jonathan Schwinge, Cloud Piercer, 2005
Plan showing the 4610-metre (15,125-foot) diameter wave breaker in the Thames Estuary.

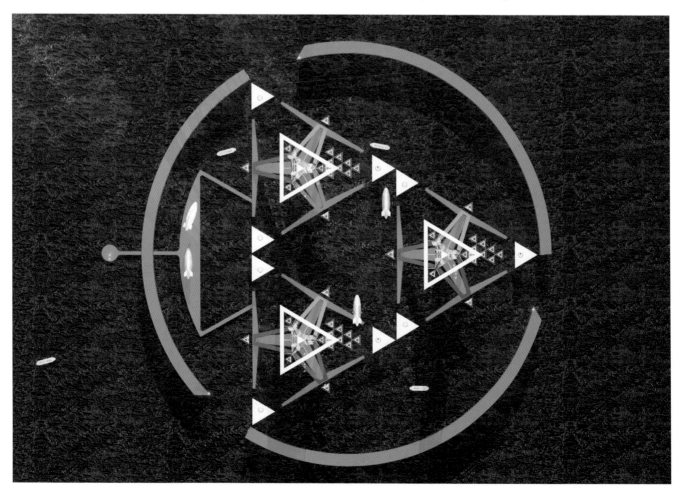

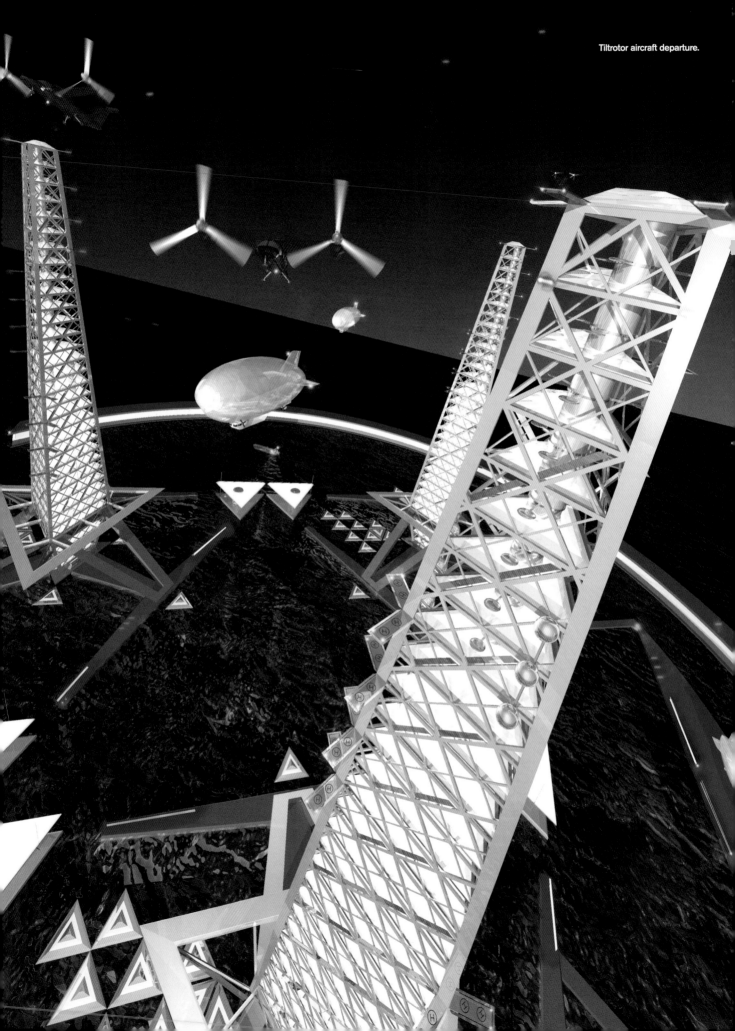

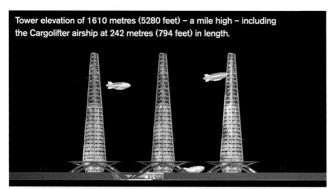

Tower elevation of 1610 metres (5280 feet) – a mile high – including the Cargolifter airship at 242 metres (794 feet) in length.

View from the inhabited wave breaker forming the protected harbour-to-ocean location.

Each tower is also divided into 32 'urban villages' arranged around service and rapid vertical-transit cores. These villages would be multi-use, in a constant process of periodic redevelopment, supporting all the activities expected of a city. A large, detached triangular deck above the structural tripod legs provides an external aerial space for leisure activities, combined with areas of parkland or sports facilities. The prime and prestigious areas at the top of each tower are large social spaces for special events, celebrations and tourists, providing a giant viewing platform over the Thames Estuary with the old city in the distance.

The plan is triangulated and tapers up and down from the structural tripod. Further triangulation of the diamond-grid lattice structure runs externally, linked to three lower 30-metre (98-foot) diameter cores that transfer to a singular upper core. On each of the 32 serviceable decks, the accommodation is built up to eight storeys, with open external spaces and articulated climatic facades incorporated as each level requires, changing over time as the villages are adapted by users. There are no deep floor plates – only glazed enclosures around subsidiary structures containing modularised buildings, intermediate platforms and open landscapes.

The lattice structure and separate villages grouped around the cores are open to the air and daylight, which also reduces wind loads and controls turbulence. The development allows for tidal power generation in the estuary, with wind turbines on the superstructure, but at individual villages a range of technologies could be upgraded in shorter time frames, including combined heat and power plants, heat exchangers, hydrogen fuel cells and related photovoltaic installations, rainwater collection systems, and natural ventilation within sheltered and landscaped sky

courts. Fire protection, thermal insulation and corrosion protection are as developed for offshore industries. Means of maintenance, refit and reconfiguration are provided at each deck level with integral craneage and massive service elevators.

Key features (per tower):
- Height: 1610 metres (5280 feet)
- Length of longest side of equilateral triangle: 330 metres (1080 feet)
- Length of shortest side of equilateral triangle: 95 metres (310 feet)
- Length of longest side of triangular deck: 770 metres (2530 feet)
- Weight: 6.5 million tonnes approx (calculation by Toby at TALL engineers)
- Capacity: approximately 3.5 million square metres (37.67 million square ft), assuming 50 per cent deck coverage with an average of eight floors on each of the 32 individually mass-damped decks.
- A further 500,000 square metres (5.38 million square feet) of shared open space is provided across the 32 decks.
- Population: approximately 90,000, but this will vary considerably depending on patterns of use and user mobility.

As a three-tower cluster and inhabited harbour, Cloud Piercer represents a potential development of between 15 million and 18 million square metres (160 and 190 square feet) of accommodation and shared open space, to form the required destination at a transport interchange on the eastern end of a maglev shuttle to old London – shrinking the extremities of the Thames Gateway to a 20-minute commuting distance via a new international airport. ∆

Mid-level tiltrotor aircraft launch platform.

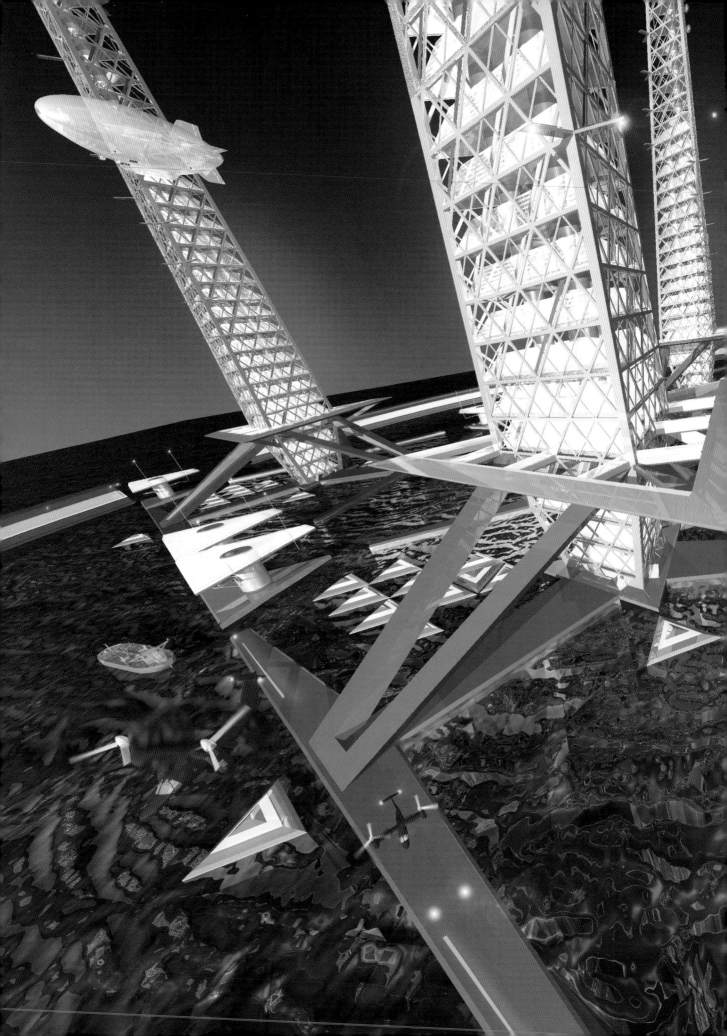

Tiltrotor pilot's view on arrival at Cloud Piercer. The sheer scale of this proposal is enormous in terms of size and structural forces. As a comparison, the ship shown in the bottom right of the image is of a similar length to that of the Canary Wharf tower, London, of 235 metres (770 feet). Next to the mile-high towers this should provide a mega-understanding of the enormity of such a project. The buildings are also permeable to reduce massive wind loadings.

Architecture with Legs

Dreaming of developing the Thames Estuary, **Ian Abley** and **Jonathan Schwinge** went to see the Maunsell Sea Forts, built off the coast of Herne Bay, Kent, in 1942. Here they met members of Project Redsand, a charitable organisation that aims to preserve the forts as a public museum, and which has so far received encouragement from both industry and government departments.

The Maunsell Sea Forts silhouetted against the three mile-high towers of Jonathan Schwinge's Cloud Piercer hypothetical project for the Thames Estuary.

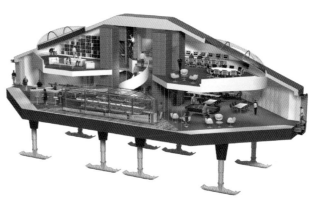

Hugh Broughton Architects and Faber Maunsell, winning proposal for modular Halley VI Research Station, 2005
Cutaway sections of the central and science modules of the British Antarctic Survey's forthcoming research station in Antarctica, and an impression of how the modules will connect to stand on the ice shelf.

The winner, in July 2005, of the British Antarctic Survey (BAS) competition to design the Halley VI Research Station in Antarctica,[1] which attracted 86 entries worldwide after its launch in June 2004 through the Royal Institute of British Architects (RIBA),[2] was the team of Faber Maunsell[3] and Hugh Broughton Architects.[4] Located 16,000 kilometres (10,000 miles) from the UK, the station will be situated on the 150-metre (490-feet) thick floating Brunt Ice Shelf, which moves 400 metres (1300 feet) per annum towards the sea. Snow accumulation means that snow levels rise by over a metre (3 feet) every year, and the sun does not rise above the horizon for three months during the Austral winter. The Halley VI will be a series of interconnecting and reconfigurable pods on a series of mechanical legs on skis that enable it to stay above the surface of the ice and be relocated inland to minimise the risk of loss due to future ice-shelf calving events.

The basis of the brief was that the research station would have minimal environmental impact on Antarctica's pristine environment. The other point about the brief is, of course, that to withstand extreme winds and freezing winter temperatures down to −56°C (−133°F), the Halley VI station is designed to ensure the most extreme environment on the planet has minimal impact upon the 16 people working there during the winter and the 52 in the summer.

The triumph of the design team's ingenuity is that they have achieved both. It has become a cliché that architects and engineers say of their projects they are elevated on legs 'to touch the ground lightly'. This is a weak justification for the designer's ability to deal with the forces of nature when designing the manmade environment, when the bigger requirement, acute in the Antarctic, is to overcome the ground conditions. As with the performance of most buildings in environments more benign than Antarctica, the emphasis has shifted to saving energy on a planet awash with the stuff, while the task of making sure that occupants are comfortable and find the building convenient seems at best secondary.

The requirement to subordinate our comfort and convenience in pursuit of sustainability has achieved such moral weight that putting the occupants first is considered mutinous in the war to save the planet from human self-interest. As in war, the ideology of sustainability expects that personal hardship is required for some greater, remote and ill-defined goal, and human ingenuity is bent to that end.

In the UK and Europe, Faber Maunsell employs over 2000 people at 28 locations as part of the AECOM Technology Corporation, a worldwide provider of professional financial and technical services that has a total of 18,000 employees in over 60 countries around the world. This is an army devoted to protecting the environment that Guy Ansell Maunsell, a star engineer of his day, might have enjoyed commanding. Born in Srinagar, Kashmir, in 1884, Guy Maunsell's father was a lieutenant-colonel in the Indian Army who sent him to be educated in England at Eastbourne College. Maunsell decided he wanted to be a civil engineer, and studied at Imperial College London, passing with honours. In 1909 he got a job with Easton Gibb and Sons Ltd on the contract to construct the Rosyth Naval Base in Scotland. He was promoted and, joining R Thorburn & Sons, he undertook the construction of several explosives factories in Scotland and Wales. In 1917 Maunsell was called up for military service and served in the trenches as a commissioned officer in the Royal Engineers, until he was recalled to construct reinforced concrete tugs and ships at a site in Shoreham by Sea, Sussex. This lasted until the end of the war, when he then took up work with the Ministry of Transport under Sir Alexander Gibb.

Maunsell worked in contracting abroad during the interwar years on massive civil engineering projects, but when hostilities broke out again in 1939, he was in charge, jointly with Gibb, for the overseeing of many secret projects. These ranged from the Thames Estuary army and naval sea forts, and the army sea forts of the Mersey Estuary, to

The postwar period saw Guy Maunsell at the firm of Maunsell, Posford and Pavry in 1952, becoming one of four founding partners of the new firm of G Maunsell and Partners in 1955. He was involved in the construction of the first North Sea exploration rig for the National Coal Board, which not only completed its task, but was then sold to Trinity House to act as a lighthouse. Maunsell was to die in 1961, from a heart attack, aged 77, unrecognised by the government for his wartime work.

concrete bombardment towers for the Normandy invasion and reinforced-concrete flush-deck freighters to bring in supplies from America without being detected by the German U-boats. It is the army forts at Redsands, similar to those at Shimmering Sands, and both in the Thames Estuary, that we visited to see first-hand in their still structurally sound picturesque state of dilapidation. In the 1960s the forts inspired Archigram when colonised by Pirate Radio in defiance of the BBC, and are a good example of what Reyner

Frank R Turner, sitting in front of architects Pamela Charlick (left) and Natasha Nicholson (right), is a historian working on Project Redsand, and has written numerous booklets about the Maunsell Forts. He lectures, is currently preparing a booklet on Guy Maunsell, and will be pleased to provide a full explanation of how the forts were built.

Banham termed *mégastructures trouvées,* along with oil rigs, submarines or the structures of the space programme.[5]

The postwar period saw Guy Maunsell at the firm of Maunsell, Posford and Pavry in 1952, becoming one of four founding partners of the new firm of G Maunsell and Partners in 1955. He was involved in the construction of the first North Sea exploration rig for the National Coal Board, which not only completed its task, but was then sold to Trinity House to act as a lighthouse. Maunsell was to die in 1961, from a heart attack, aged 77, unrecognised by the government for his wartime work.

As senior partner (1959–80), John Baxter expanded G Maunsell from a 45-strong UK practice to an international force of more than 2000, excelling in bridge design and transportation, including the Westway in London. Baxter himself acknowledged that the project was conceived and built in an era when engineering was carried out on a 'decide, announce, defend' basis, with little or no local consultation. In 1976, he confessed that it had marked the beginning of the anti-roads campaign, encouraged by Michael Heseltine, then Junior Transport Minister, who had rescripted his speech at the last minute, excising praise for the engineers and planners in favour of a pledge to help those living in the structure's shadow. Baxter was president of the Institution of Civil Engineers that year.[6] The Northway, Southway and Eastway were scrapped, and a Conservative administration fuelled the anti-car prejudice that underpins New Labour planning policies today.

Regardless of how interminable public consultation proves to be at the moment, major infrastructural development is objected to unless it has minimal environmental impact – which, except for a temporary installation like the Halley VI station in the Antarctic, is an impossible brief. Architects and engineers need to find their own legs when it comes to confronting the fearful 'do nothing' sentiment of sustainability. We have a planet to develop. Δ

Notes
1. www.antarctica.ac.uk, accessed 30 July 2005.
2. www.riba.org/go/RIBA/News/ Press_3293.html, accessed 29 June 2004.
3. www.fabermaunsell.com, accessed 8 August 2005.
4. www.hbarchitects.co.uk, accessed 8 August 2005.
5. Reyner Banham, *Megastructure: Urban Futures of the Recent Past,* Thames and Hudson (London), 1976, p 28.
6. Andrew Mylius, 'John Baxter – The Man Who Masterminded London's Most Hated Road', *The Guardian,* 10 November 2003. www.guardian.co.uk/transport/ Story/0,2763,1081367,00.html, accessed 08 August 2005.

Acknowledgements
With additional material courtesy of Frank R Turner (pictured above), and thanks to Robin Adcroft at Project Redsand: www.project-redsand.com.

Standing Tall in the Estuary

Accompanied by the guest-editors of this issue, **Natasha Nicholson** and **Pamela Charlick** take an exhilarating ride beyond the Thames Estuary, off the coast of Herne Bay, on *Bayblast*, the rigid hull inflatable boat (RHIB) – a trip that takes in the impressive Kentish Flats wind farm, under construction, and the Maunsell Forts. With substantial-scale projects already nestled in the estuary, new possibilities for architectural interpretation can be thrown up for the Thames Gateway flood plain. However, what potential contribution might the wind farm also make to the area in terms of power generation?

Three of the 30 Kentish Flats wind-farm turbines, arranged in a grid, with the Maunsell Sea Forts in the background.

Bayblast, a rigid hull inflatable boat (RHIB), operates from Herne Bay and Whitstable and can take up to 12 passengers (www.bayblast.co.uk).

Kentish Flats is the third of the UK's large-scale offshore wind farms. Situated 8.5 km (5 miles) from land in the shallow waters off the north Kent coast, it will provide up to 90 megawatts (MW) of energy from 30 wind turbines.

From the seafront at Herne Bay, the 70-metre (230-foot) high posts appear as a succession of smudges above the horizon line. But when you get up close to them the scale of the installation is impressive. We were there when the *Sea Energy* crane ship was preparing to hoist another vast turbine head into position.

Each of the 500-tonne (550-ton) wind turbines is erected in several stages. A 40-metre (130-foot) long cylindrical steel monopile of 4 metres (13 feet) diameter is rammed into the seabed using a pile driver mounted on an installation vessel with six jack legs. Then a 'transition piece' is attached to the top of the monopile – bright yellow for visibility to shipping – and with ladder and platform for service access. Finally, each component of the wind turbine is craned into position: the tower, the 'nacelle' (containing the gearbox, generator and 'controller') and the three 45-metre (145-foot) long rotor blades. The components are transported to the site by sea from the preassembly facility at Felixstowe.

A network of buried submarine cables link across the 700 metres (2300 feet) between the foundations of each turbine to create this 'green' power station that connects into the National Grid via an onshore substation at Herne Bay. The turbines are unmanned. They are remotely controlled and monitored by an onshore computer-based control system, and designed to need little maintenance – just two annual service inspections. Once commissioned, the turbines' computer controls the operation of the system to optimise performance. It will monitor wind speed and direction, and turn the rotors to face into the wind. And it will stop the rotors if wind speeds are either too high or too low.

The Kentish Flats wind farm has a projected 20-year lifespan, after which Elsam A/S, the Danish energy company and developer, plans to disassemble and remove the existing components. However, it may be possible to reuse the existing infrastructure and upgrade the turbines.

Smart, green, nonpolluting technology in the windiest country in Europe sounds like a good formula. But what will the Kentish Flats wind farm produce in terms of energy?

The calculation to convert the rated capacity of the array of turbines (MW) into power (KWh/year) is as follows: 30 (number of turbines) x 3MW (rating of individual turbine) x 24 (hours in day) x 365 (days in year) x 0.35 (average capacity factor of turbine due to intermittency) x 1000 (to convert MWh to kWh)[1] This 90-MW array will produce up to 275,940,000 KW/h in a year. Based on a figure of 4400 KWh/year average electricity consumption per British household, the wind farm would provide for around 62,700 households.

The British Wind Energy Association (BWEA) publishes a figure of 70,000 'annual homes equivalent' for Kentish Flats.[2]

Elsam A/S publishes a figure of 100,000 British households against annual output of 280 million KWh for Kentish Flats, which equates to an average consumption of 2800 KWh/year per household.[3] Although this is reasonable for electrical consumption (lights and appliances only) in a household using gas heating and built to 2002 Building Regulations standards, it is very low as a UK average.

To put this into context, 10 per cent of current electricity supply in the UK, which in 2004 was 375,000 GWh, could be provided by 135 similar wind farms in addition to the Kentish Flats.[4]

The UK is primed for a surge in the development of renewable technologies in order to meet its commitments for reductions in carbon dioxide (CO_2) emissions and to address concerns about the security of future energy supplies as the UK depends increasingly on imported energy. The target of 60 per cent reduction in CO_2 emissions by around 2050 is a tough proposition. Key elements in the strategy must be cleaner sources of energy combined with increased energy efficiency. Reducing overall consumption should be an aspiration, but it is far from becoming reality. In the domestic household and transport sectors, electricity consumption remains on a firmly upward trend.

In 2004, renewables provided 3.6 per cent of the electricity generated in the UK.[5] Government targets are for 10 per cent of electricity from renewable sources by 2010, and 20 per cent by 2020. Wind is seen as a competitively priced technology offering the best opportunity for fast, large-scale development.

The government's 2003 Energy White Paper *Our Energy Future – Creating a Low Carbon Economy,* set out a vision for energy production in 2020 based on more diversity of sources of supply, including large-scale offshore wind farms. 'The backbone of the electricity system will still be a market-based grid, balancing the supply of large power stations. But some of those large power stations will be offshore marine plants, including wave, tidal and wind farms.'[6]

Danish energy company and developer Elsam A/S has a superb website (www.kentishflats.co.uk) showing the construction of the Kentish Flats wind farm in 2005. The two images here show the scale of the monopiles, and the turbine head being lifted from the crane ship before the third blade is installed.

This launched the UK government's development initiative for offshore wind farms, assisted by a capital grant programme, and there has been no shortage of suitable sites in shallow waters around the coast that meet the requirements: high wind speeds, suitable seabed conditions, access to grid connections and sufficient distance from sensitive habitats. Offshore wind farms are more expensive, and they suffer from electrical transmission losses. However, they are increasingly more competitive because of energy outputs up to 25 per cent higher than on land, the opportunities of advances in wind turbine technology, such as 4.5-MW offshore turbines, and generally fewer problems obtaining consents than for their onshore equivalents.

Most of the wind-farm sites fall within the 12 nautical mile territorial limit, which means that the land – the seabed – is owned by the Crown Estate. The Crown Estate Commissioners do not have powers as a planning authority or statutory regulator, but they do have the power to grant the 23-year leases for development, operation and decommissioning of the wind farms. Under the Crown Estate Act they also have a duty to maintain and enhance the capital value of the estate and the income obtained from it.

Projects currently seeking development consents are increasingly ambitious in scale. The London Array is planned for a shallow-water site on sandbanks in the Thames Estuary, between the two major shipping lanes to the Port of London. With a capacity of 1,000 MW from up to 270 turbines over an area of up to 245 square kilometres (94 square miles), it will displace existing fishing grounds and impact on the feeding grounds of red-throated divers. However, a number of projects of this size, and larger, are likely to be realised, and will have a real impact on the balance of UK energy production.

Shifting in scale to the complex system for national energy production and distribution presents further new challenges. The often cited 'problem' of intermittency of supply affects many renewable energy sources, including wind. We could not source all our energy from renewables, because sometimes the lights would go out. It is generally accepted that the existing National Grid will be able to accommodate the fluctuations in supply if up to 20 per cent of UK energy supply is provided by intermittent renewables. The network already has to accommodate substantial peaks and troughs in consumer demand.

However, research at the Environmental Change Institute (ECI) in Oxford has shown that, with the right mix of renewable energy supplies, the standby capacity in power stations can be reduced to acceptably low levels, and a renewable portfolio of up to 50 per cent of total supply could be achieved over the next 20 years. Graham Sinden, of ECI, proposes a mix of 20 per cent from wind-, 15 per cent from wave- and 5 per cent from tidal power, with a further 10 per cent sourced from solar, biomass, landfill and domestic combined heat and power (dCHP).[7] The key is balancing energy sources that peak and trough in different conditions, and also distributing the sources of supply as widely as possible, which means more smaller sites, rather than a few large ones. This will help to maintain reliable supplies with minimum variability.

In this future scenario, the Kentish Flats wind farm will be seen as a pioneering project from the days when just 1 per cent of UK electricity supplies came from the wind. The controlled development of offshore wind farms must be an important part of this future, but this will have to be in parallel with the vigorous implementation of other renewable-energy technologies. ◬

Notes

1. Friends of the Earth, Greenpeace and the World Wildlife Fund (WWF), yes2wind, http://yes2wind.com/ faq.html, accessed 4 August 2005.
2. www.bwea.com/offshore/ round1. html, accessed 4 August 2005.
3. www.kentishflats.co.uk, accessed 4 August 2005.
4. Department of Trade and Industry, *UK Energy Sector Indicators 2005*, p 38. www.dti.gov.uk, accessed 4 August 2005.
5. Ibid, p 17.
6. Department of Trade and Industry, *Our Energy Future – Creating a Low Carbon Economy*, TSO (London), 2003. www.dti.gov.uk/energy/whitepaper/ index.shtml, accessed 6 August 2005.
7. www.eci.ox.ac.uk/lowercf/ intermittency/renewables.html, accessed 4 August 2005.

Mega-Rural: Made in Sunderland

Jonathan Schwinge anticipates habitation spheres, manufactured like ships from vast modular subassemblies. Floated from covered yards on pontoons, they are airlifted for segmental delivery anywhere in the world by fleets of high-capacity freight airships from the leading civilian and military logistics companies. A new market, perhaps, for old shipyards, like Pallion shipyard in Jonathan's family home town of Sunderland.

Originally from London, as a teenager I lived in Sunderland in the northeast of England, occasionally visiting decommissioning shipyards, de-anodising and reconstructing the aluminium-spoked wheels on my BMX bicycle. Then I would ride to the Wear to view the last remaining manmade megastructural tankers having their enormous superstructures craned into position, with vast teams of suspended overhead welders in full engagement. This undoubtedly fired my interest in advanced materials and processes from marine and aeronautics engineering, tempered by my disillusionment with the poor-spec, can't-do nature of the construction industry.

Mega-rural would be designed for sequential manufacture in former shipbuilding areas, for distribution nationally or for export. A personal aim is to reinvigorate the semi-redundant supersized enclosed Pallion dry dock on the river Wear in Sunderland. Closed in 1988, after six centuries of shipbuilding

Indicative view of Mega-Rural housing project being constructed from Pallion shipyard, Sunderland, 2005.

Potential enclosed building facility for Mega-Rural housing.

in the region, but currently operating on ship repair and small fabrication, Pallion would offer an excellent manufacturing platform.

Like water droplets spread across the landscape, each spherical Mega-rural apartment unit can 'dock' with existing towns and villages within the existing B-road network through peripheral farmland and woodland. Clustered in the countryside, the spheres could equally be used to create new settlements, or be distributed along the fringes of other transport infrastructure.

The remote spheres have central lifts and servicing, and are elevated on two legs with footpads for minimal interruption of the surrounding landscape at ground level. The land is a communal amenity, or farmed for seasonal 'energy crops', either for use as biomass or to be fermented for the production of hydrogen for use in fuel cells.

The central core and atria arrangement feature subassemblies for small retail, such as a 'cornershop' for milk and newspapers, a post office, farm shop, bakery or café, with kindergarten and after-school modules all as 'standard options' in the product range. Further 'social spheres' might be identified within the rural setting, for gymnasia, swimming pools, restaurants, bingo, bars and cinema.

Key features:
- Module weights optimised for the airship delivery and installation system – the German Cargolifter, attempting to come out of receivership, aimed for a payload of 160 tonnes (176 tons), but other systems in the UK, America, France and China anticipate different payloads

Final superproduct for habitation.

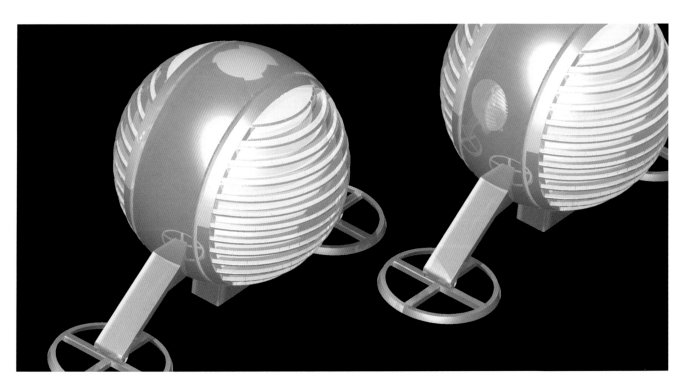

- Sphere radius: 62 metres (203 feet)
- Overall height: 70 metres (230 feet)
- Foot-to-foot spread: 125 metres (410 feet)
- Machine room – fewer lifts fitted after installation
- 12 storeys with high floor-to-soffit heights for secondary mezzanine levels, and bathroom, toilet or kitchen pods
- Underground access and car parking from neighbouring villages.

Specification:
- Aluminium semi-monocoque construction
- Vacuum insulation panels from the refrigeration container industry
- Contratherm Syntactic Phenolic Foam fire protection and corrosion protection from the demanding offshore oil and gas industries
- Supergloss and superdurable aviation and yacht industry coatings
- Solar-reflecting glazing using automotive industry lamination technology.
- Eco-tech: energy crops (elephant grass planted around spheres), geothermal soil energy for heating and cooling, fuel cell hydrogen energy and natural ventilation.

Mega-rural would need to be an unprecedented exercise in technology transfer, and dependent on an order stream for the repetitive building type. The European Space Agency (ESA) technology-transfer programme describes technology transfer as: 'The process of using technology, expertise, know-how or facilities for a purpose not originally intended by the developing organisation. Technology transfer implies that a technology developed for one sector is then used in a totally different area.'[1] Martin Pawley, in *Theory and Design in the Second Machine Age*, similarly describes this as 'the process whereby the techniques and materials developed in one creative field, industry or culture are adapted to serve in other creative fields, industries or cultures'.[2]

The transfer of new and advanced technology from one industry to another can have enormous cost burdens for the initiating military, space, aviation, marine and automotive performance sectors with funding needed for scientists and technicians, laboratories, research and development, testing, lead timing, marketing, manufacturing capabilities and product market absorption. The transferred receptor field or industry – in this case architecture – takes full advantage of the lightened cost and time burden on the preproduction stages. There is a truly parasitical yet beneficial advantage for the slow-moving construction industry. The benefit of the relationship to architecture is heightened building performance. The fact is that architecture has no R&D department. It has to borrow one, and advanced sectors are a technological force waiting to be used.

The exchange and implementation of new technologies from advanced sectors is strongly supported as the

The dusk falls over the 'energy crop' in which the two supergloss black Mega-Rural apartment spheres stand, having been delivered and installed the previous growing season by a 242-metre (794-foot) Cargolifter airship, seen in the distance.

'commercialisation of technology', as performance technology manufacturers are keen to yield a profitable return on their investment, and are quick to recognise both 'technology push' and 'market pull'. The technologically slower industry of land architecture is beginning to realise the availability of advanced materials and methods of construction, with a few highly aware individuals becoming appliers of technology or, to use a NASA term, 'transfer agents', within construction. They attempt to gain a better understanding of the potential of 'bits of useful kit' to enhance the performance and aesthetic of their buildings.

In contrast, NASA has dedicated agencies in the form of US national and regional technology-transfer centres to facilitate partnering with industry, and to introduce its technological space and aviation solutions. RTI International, a NASA partner for the commercialisation of technologies into civilian industry, is 'Bringing Technology from Space to the Marketplace.'[3] The Innovative Technology Transfer Partnerships (ITTP) programme 'serves all NASA Enterprises and supports their missions by facilitating the development of new technologies through partnerships with US industry'.[4] After the historic flight of the Wright brothers in December 1903, the US Congress established NASA 'to supervise and direct

the scientific study of the problems of flight, with a view to their solution'. The 1958 Space Act stipulated that NASA's vast body of scientific and technical knowledge also benefit mankind. A hundred years after the Wright brothers, the intention to transfer technology seems limited to the US, as the director of NASA's ITTP Benjamin Neumann aims to 'ensure that the benefits of the space program are used to improve the quality of life of Americans, and the competitiveness of US industry'.[5]

In the UK there sadly appears to be no serious effort to transfer manufacturing technology systematically into architectural production, whether for the benefit of British industry, or for the wider benefit of mankind. Mega-rural remains optimistic, while Pallion stands mostly idle. ∆

Notes
1. www.esa.int/SPECIALS/ Technology_Transfer/SEMLYSRMD6E_ 0.html, accessed 8 August 2005.
2. Martin Pawley, *Theory and Design in the Second Machine Age,* Basil Blackwell (Oxford), 1990, p 140.
3. www.rti.org, accessed 4 August 2005.
4. NASA, *Innovative Technology Transfer Partnerships, 2004 Program*:
www.nasa.gov/pdf/1982main_ partnerships. pdf, accessed 8 August 2005.
5. Benjamin Neumann, 'Introduction', *NASA Aeronautics News,* Vol 5, Issue 1, February/March 2004. www.aerospace.nasa.gov/events/ news/vol5_iss1/neumann.htm, accessed 8 August 2005.

Mass Customisation and the Manufactured Module

James Woudhuysen, Professor of Forecasting
and Innovation at De Montfort University,
and co-author of *Why is Construction So
Backwards?* (Wiley-Academy, 2004), talks
to **Stephen Kieran** and **James Timberlake**
of KieranTimberlake Architects about how
they are setting out to refabricate architecture.

The European Commissioner for
External Trade, Peter Mandelson, looks
around the modular triumph of the
A380 Airbus.

Reading *Refabricating Architecture* is a joy. When so much
divides America from Europe, or at least appears to divide the
two, here are the principals of KieranTimberlake Associates LLP,
Philadelphia, upholding transatlantic unity. They explain how,
in 2013, a notional Boeing Worldwide Constructs factory, based
on the firm's 38-hectare (95-acre), 11-storey room in Everett,
Washington, could airlift massive subassemblies of buildings to
global destinations – with the help of Airbus jets.

Ah, those subassemblies. 'The more one attempts to
undertake at the point of assembly,' the authors note, 'the more
difficult it is to control quality'.[1] *Refabricating Architecture* is a
confident, vivid and irrefutable case for moving construction
into the world of supply-chain management, upgradable services
and buildings as quilts, with hardly any joints to be made on site.

The book is also a paean to IT. Historically, architecture has
relied on flat drawings to convey a construction – plans,
sections, elevations and details. These 2-D representations of 3-D
buildings would be better simulated: 'Simulation makes possible
the fragmentation of large artefacts, such as aircraft, into large,
integrated components that can be fabricated anywhere in the
world and brought together for final assembly.'[2]

I wondered what practical experiences had made Stephen
Kieran and James Timberlake write the book, and how it had
been received in the US.

'From the beginning,' says Timberlake, 'our practice has been
based in craft, and in construction, and the careful integration
of the two. Over the past decade we'd become disappointed with
the level of quality of the craft, as executed: not only our own,
but within architecture at large.'

In response to this, at the University of Pennsylvania, where
they run a final-semester Master of Architecture design research
laboratory, the partnership began exploring ways to increase
architectural quality through the integration of disciplines
around new materials and methods. In late 2000, they wrote a
proposal to the College of Fellows of the American Institute of
Architects. The college was sponsoring, for the first time ever, a
research fellowship – the Benjamin Latrobe Research Fellowship.

Kieran and Timberlake won that first fellowship, and decided
then to write up their research in a document that eventually
became *Refabricating Architecture*. From the start, the intention
was to write theory based on the current, factual state of
architecture and construction. The authors wanted to instigate
change, and in that spirit *Refabricating Architecture* has been
enthusiastically received within academic circles.

But what about their theory as it applies to their everyday
practice?

'We are now beginning to see the architecture profession and
the construction industry pick it up,' continued Timberlake,
justifiably proud. 'It has resonated among some in the
development community, where monetary carrying costs can be
the difference between doing a project and shelving it. And like
Why is Construction So Backward?, we wanted to prompt
changes within the profession. Both of our books begin at the
same place, but take quite different patterns to the end. We
both seek better craft, quality, and design. We are in agreement
that under the present design, supply, construction and
procurement arrangements, without change, architecture and
construction face a regressive future and more disappointment
rather than success.'[3]

Architecture needs to think bigger when it comes to
modules, and develop the logistical means for handling them.
Kieran and Timberlake have realised that although cars, planes
and ships move through space, buildings, which will always
remain relatively static artefacts even after delivery and
installation as manufactured modules, are often smaller. They
ask: Why can't buildings go through the kind of giant-scale
modular assembly processes that exist at Kvaerner's
Philadelphia shipyard?

As a practice, KieranTimberlake Associates is obviously
influenced by the successes and ambitious scope of US transport
design. So why had they omitted to consider techniques for
manufacturing railway trains?

In fact, they love trains, and wish Amtrak had selected a
manufacturer from Europe with a proven design rather than

THE NEW CLIENT MANDATE *The design and execution of architecture is increasingly subject to a new rule of economy. Architects find themselves having to increase quality and scope disproportionately to the execution cost and time consumed. Clients are demanding more for less.*

Image from *Refabricating Architecture*, courtesy of Kieran and Timberlake.

specifying and procuring a design inferior to that of rolling stock in Europe. The focus of *Refabricating Architecture* on automobile, aircraft and shipping manufacturers was partly, according to Timberlake, to do with 'ease of access to the plants, to people and processes. Also, the three reinforce our argument about scalability – sheer size and numbers. And they exhibit nice differences in supply-chain characteristics, modalities and assembly methods.'

In any case, there are only so many arguments you can handle at once. 'Folks criticise our book for instancing the automobile industry, because they believe it represents mass production rather than mass customisation. In reply, we hold up the wonderful example of Bentley cars. They are truly bespoke – we love that word – and so clearly represent mass customisation. Train manufacturing has the scale, and some of the processes, but we weren't sure that it truly represented the best examples of the theory we were trying to explain.'

I said I thought Bentley cars were an example of customisation without the preface 'mass', but we soon moved on.

One of the great things Kieran and Timberlake do is ridicule those who say that manufacturing methodologies are a pipe dream as far as construction is concerned. I like the way they attack previous attempts in the genre as 'automating mediocrity'. But, allowing for poetic licence, how do they reply to sceptics who don't believe that US industry will make the advances suggested by 2013? As the pair hint, US off-site fabrication, in giving the world the concept of 'trailer trash', has done neither itself nor the domain of housing any favours.

'US construction has a long way to go, and 2013, seven years from now, might be optimistic,' confided Timberlake. 'Unlike the manufacturing models we chose, construction is highly fragmented, from the supply chain through to procurement. Of course, too, the design profession is separated from the construction industry – unlike the manufacturers with

integrated design capabilities we focused upon. Last, the US government is disinclined to involve itself in private companies or industry, so there is little impetus for change from the government, unlike, for instance, the UK or Japan. The US modular housing industry is clearly behind many Japanese and European manufacturers in terms of CAD/CAM, integration and production.'

Kieran and Timberlake are optimistic, however. They are keen on several bright stars in the construction industry:

- Skanska, which has experience in Europe with offsite technologies[4]
- CAPSYS, a company building multifamily prototypes in Brooklyn New York shipyard[5]
- Kullman Industries, New Jersey, which builds ambassadorial outposts for the US State Department off site, and ships them round the world[6]
- Jacobs Engineering, in Charleston, South Carolina, which, with high-quality off-site techniques, fabricates upmarket clean laboratories – also for shipment worldwide.[7]

Each of these examples is helping to change how the US and international construction industries will act, think and produce. But Kieran and Timberlake are a little too quick to abandon mass production as 'the ideal of the early twentieth century'. They assert that mass customisation 'is the recently emerged reality of the twenty-first century,' and argue that this is cultural production rather than the making of industrial outputs.[8] By cultural production they mean that, rather than decide among options produced by industry, the customer 'determines what the options will be by participating in the flow of the design process from the very start'.[9]

I agree with them that the advances of Dell are fantastic, although no other computer manufacturers have been able to emulate its ability to tailor PCs to what buyers ask for. Kieran and Timberlake also know the book *Digital Design and Manufacturing*. That book seems to be more accurate when it prefers the term 'personalisation' to 'customisation'. With personalisation, buyers are able to choose configurations only from options that have been predetermined by manufacturers.[10]

In response, Timberlake again cites Bentley,[11] adding to this the BMW Z4.[12] He insists that 'the first is true mass customisation; the second is an example of design integration, with possibilities for late changes in the production stream. Both occur within industries that are upheld as paragons of mass production, not customisation.'

Warming to this theme, he continued: 'Our communication software, our CAD abilities, and the supply-chain opportunities all exist to enable true mass customisation to occur, which we think *Digital Design and Manufacturing* ignores. And isn't personalisation really another way of saying mass customisation?

'The existing construction industry already applies mass-customisation techniques to integrated component assemblies –

bathrooms, kitchens, curtain walls, mechanical/electrical system components. These assemblies allow architects to customise or personalise the component for integration into a larger architectural composition. The Permasteelisa Group,[13] a global curtain-wall manufacturer based in the Veneto, Italy, deploys components from worldwide manufacturers, custom assembled to the specifications of the architects whose designs it executes. It integrates engineering, design and manufacturing to ensure high-end final products that look unique to each project, but in fact use many standard smaller bits within the kit supplied.'

Myself, I remain more convinced that personalisation is how the mass market tends to operate. I don't find anything especially cultural about architects abdicating responsibility for design decisions to customers. This plea for customer- and user-led design is all too familiar from the world of IT, and fails to convince. Although the phrase 'master builder' is too loaded, Kieran and Timberlake are much nearer the mark when observing that: 'Today, through the agency of information management tools, the architect can once again become the master builder by integrating the skills and intelligences at the core of architecture.'[14]

To be fair, Timberlake was adamant that the duo don't want to abdicate design responsibility. Rather, 'the opportunities for making adjustments, and program revisions, and final improvements, which in the past have notoriously stopped the design and production show, can now be an integral part of the process.

'We do advocate the return of authority and responsibility for design and control to the architect, as it once was, in the role of "master controller". We don't think we will be master builders again, at least in the sense of Brunelleschi 500 years ago. But by embracing integration, collective intelligence and the technological tools available to us, architects can regain the kind of control of processes they have not enjoyed for nearly a century.'

There are other nuances in *Refabricating Architecture* that I wanted Kieran and Timberlake to justify: for example, their view that the making of architecture is 'organised chaos'.[15] Sometimes it seems that they nod approvingly, but in my view rather eclectically, to the doctrines of chaos and complexity. There is no need to try to dignify a rational case for modular subassemblies with these somewhat overblown ideas, wrenched from unrelated scientific domains.[16]

'Well, chaos and complexity are in our recent past, in that Robert Venturi and Denise Scott Brown were mentors of each of us during our early careers. Ours is less nodding approval than acknowledgement of the messy vitality the process of making architecture is ... and in comparison to the more rational processes of the three nonconstruction industries explored by *Refabricating Architecture*, architecture and construction are indeed chaotic and complex!'

For Timberlake, there are three reasons for the anarchy that obtains.

First, architecture and construction remain processes with few overlaps – design and building only rarely overlap, because of the needs of the client, time constraints and cost constraints.

Second, the fragmentation of design input adds to confusion. A multiplicity of consultants gets involved in the most basic of projects. Supplier inputs into construction, and different methods of procurement, make things worse. The result is that architecture is a nonlinear affair.

Last, Timberlake argues that, in *Why is Construction So Backward?*, Ian Abley and myself had alluded to a similar chaos and complexity, and a lack of conformity to early craft. He notes our point that, to uphold a true return to craft, construction needs to embrace new technologies and methods for making.[17] But what we meant was not craft in the sense of the present use of construction trades, so much as a turn to manufacturing architecture – whether built like ships, simulated, modularised and assembled like the A380 Airbus, or assembled like production-run cars.

My final quibble was about Kieran and Timberlake's fondness for new materials. I, too, am a fan – but Ian Abley makes the point that there is plenty to be done with old materials as much as new ones.

Timberlake accepts this. More positively, though, he adds: 'If today's new materials enable integration, lighter assemblies and new technologies, then the world of design and construction will be enhanced by embracing them, rather than ignoring their possibilities.

'There used to be a saying around the American automobile industry: "They don't make them like they used to." That was a subtle hint that older was better. In the past decade, however, with the advent of new materials, systems, assemblies, designs and technologies, automobiles have become better than ever.'

Kieran and Timberlake want to take architecture to a completely new level by embracing new materials, systems, assemblies, designs and technologies – an ambition they share with Ian Abley and myself. ∆

Notes
1. Stephen Kieran and James Timberlake, *Refabricating Architecture: How Manufacturing Methodologies are Poised to Transform Building Construction*, McGraw-Hill (New York, London), 2004, p 87.
2. Ibid, p 59.
3. James Woudhuysen and Ian Abley, *Why is Construction So Backward?*, Wiley-Academy (Chichester), 2004, p 163.
4. www.skanska.com, accessed 10 August 2005.
5. www.capsyscorp.com, accessed 10 August 2005.
6. www.kullman.com, accessed 10 August 2005.
7. www.jacobs.com, accessed 10 August 2005.
8. Kieran and Timberlake, 'Argument', *Refabricating Architecture*, op cit, p xii.
9. Ibid, p 111.
10. Daniel Schodek, Martin Bechthold, Kimo Griggs, Kenneth Martin Kao and Marco Steinberg, *Digital Design and Manufacturing: CAD/CAM Applications in Architecture and Design*, Wiley (Hoboken, New Jersey), 2004, p 156.
11. www.bentleymotors.com, accessed 10 August 2005.
12. www.bmw.com, accessed 10 August 2005.
13. www.permasteelisa.com, accessed 10 August 2005.
14. Kieran and Timberlake, op cit, p xii.
15. Ibid, p 53.
16. John Gillott and Manjit Kumar, *Science and the Retreat From Reason*, Merlin Press (London), 1995.
17. Woudhuysen and Abley, op cit, pp 258–60.

Why Drive a TT and Live in a Broken Teapot?

What is the fascination with do-it-yourself repairs and tweeness? Obviously old houses are great because they are large, and often stand in the best locations. And, of course, some old houses are the equivalent of classic cars. But most are old bangers – after several owners they are worn-out maintenance nightmares. Ian Abley asks: Why not knock them down and make way for the manufactured modular housing equivalent of an Audi TT in the gap site? A lot more demolition would result in far more interesting neighbourhoods, lower running costs, and less need for wind farms (as beautiful as they are).

Deputy Prime Minister John Prescott demanded a 'Design for Manufacture' competition for family homes costing £60,000 (excluding land). The target was met in 2005, but everyone wondered what the point was. Prescott had unintentionally marked the centenary of *Spectator* magazine's 'Cheap Cottages' competition for Letchworth. The magazine's editor, John St Loe Strachey, wanted dwellings costing £150 – and got them. In 1905 this would be the equivalent of about £11,500 today. That a 'cheap' home is five times more expensive today cannot be explained entirely by skills shortages, standards being more onerous, planning complex or community infrastructure costs, marketing, sales overheads and the house-builder's profit. It is rather that construction is the only sector in which the cost of living for the majority has not been cheapened by a century of manufacturing, which has simultaneously raised standards of living beyond the wildest dreams of 1905. The housing market is not about productivity, as a car manufacturer would approach it.

Houses are not like cars. Houses do not depreciate as do production-run cars on leaving the forecourt. If they did, we would expect houses to have a look, performance and list of features that make their loss in value worth paying for. They would be as good as an Audi TT. No one would enter a protracted financial arrangement without break clauses accepting responsibility for the dilapidation and malfunction of a depreciating dwelling designed without R&D, not made in a factory, handed over in less than perfect condition, lacking an aftercare package, and with a worthless 'guarantee'. Since houses appreciate in value while falling apart, most people sign up willingly for mortgages, or aspire to, and try coping with DIY.

Broken homes with the design content of a twee teapot are valued with land in the UK. It is possible to value land and accommodation separately, even if made of masonry. But the

UK has a government-regulated market in planning approvals on the basis of shifting architectural judgements that suggest the building is the important factor, but which is really a disguised process of conditionally reallocating to landowners development rights nationalised since 1947.

Before then, anyone could develop anywhere they owned. This used to mean property values were based on whether living somewhere was better than elsewhere. Today speculation depends on development being restricted so that usefulness and attractiveness are secondary. The clue is that, today, a house the size of a teapot, and even in bad repair, will be sought after if it is one of a sufficiently limited number of homes in relation to the legacy of old planning approvals for important land uses, like work places or schools, and the trickle of new ones.

It is a delicate process of negotiation to effectively make sure that locally, regionally and nationally there are fewer planning approvals in circulation than there are households hoping to get hold of one, to sustain the scarcity value of the entire housing stock. That rationing of development rights has proven a perfect vehicle, better than the stock market and more affordable than the art market, through which to speculate.

Government talks about increasing housing supply, and could create a surplus of planning approvals for land uses before anyone asked for them. Each existing approved suburban plot could be given automatic permission for redevelopment as up to six storeys of multi-use accommodation. But the bottom would fall out of the broken-teapot business.

Taken further, approving designs in advance of specific sites being identified, based on popular prototypes proven capable of sequential production, would challenge the laborious construction industry in the habit of treating every project as though it were prototypical. Returning to every freeholder his or her right to develop land would transform everyone into a discerning customer for buildings. Few would continue with the quaint practice of finalising architectural designs as work proceeds on putting together a collection of ill-fitting bits, delivered in the wrong order, and in all sorts of weather. In a Britain really awash with planning approvals we would appreciate that a multi-use megastructure, along with simpler and smaller prefabricated or manufactured single-use buildings, is a way of industrialising architectural production free from the limitations of the natural site.

But this prospect is subject to a range of social factors beyond the architect's professional ability to resolve through the technicalities of architectural design. No matter how much government talks of 'design for manufacture', the Treasury will have none of it. The financial fall-out from the required surfeit of planning approvals, let alone a reassertion of the meaning of freehold, would bring the government down and shake the economy.

Architecture would never be the same again. Manufacturers like Audi might gain a massive market for static architectural TTs. Every gap site in dilapidated terraces would be seen, not as a laborious task of reconstruction, but as a parking space for a manufactured home. And like cars in car transporters, some Audi homes might be fitted into a larger vehicle. That vehicle would not have to go anywhere either. It would sit there – a megastructure – in prime locations that had previously been a composition of increasingly expensive handcrafted teapots.

The Audi TT car driver who lives in that manufactured environment would, for the first time, judge architecture with the same discretion he or she had used at the car showroom. ᗺ

Triumph and Tragedy on the Home Front

The history of the prefabricated is one of complete 'nonperformance' for themost renowned designs, produced by the most famous architects. Here, **Martin Pawley** reviews *The Prefabricated Home* by Colin Davies and explains how Davies' text reconciles the production failure of seminal works such as Buckminster Fuller's Wichita House and Lloyd Wright's Usonian Houses with the Second World War's prefab boom.

Let's not beat about the bush. Let's get straight to the point. There has been an awful lot of interest in prefabrication in recent years, but not much has as yet come out of it except this book, which is a gem. *The Prefabricated Home* (Reaktion Books, 2005) should be read especially by people who have plunged into the pursuit of the £60,000 house, if only because a lot of history is gathered together here that cannot be found in one source anywhere else. History that is as bright and fresh as a minted coin, and as relevant as the Office of the Deputy Prime Minister itself.

Realising, no doubt at an early stage, that the contribution of architects to the history of prefabricated housing consists largely of photographs and obfuscatory claims and excuses for nonperformance, Davies allocates an entire chapter to an 'architectural history', which is followed by a 'non-architectural history' consisting of a brisk run through the engineering and contracting contribution, and which makes for a grim comparison. Richard Buckminster Fuller's 1945 Wichita House, for example, an architectural standby for the last 80 years, has remained singular throughout its life, despite having (so it was said) no less than 3700 already ordered 'off the drawing board' by would-be owners.

Richard Rogers, Zip-Up, 1968.

Other architect designs for prefabricated dwellings 'chosen to be canonized and celebrated, mainly because they were designed by famous architects, were all complete failures by any objective, non-architectural measure,' says Davies. He includes in this category Le Corbusier's Maison Citrohan, Konrad Wachsmann's Packaged House designs with Walter Gropius, the work of Jean Prouvé, and even Frank Lloyd Wright and his Usonian Houses, because of the tiny numbers of each of them that were ever built. The victor in this gloomy contest is Walter Gropius and his General Panel House, endlessly modified but never put into production. Nonetheless, in the world of architecture it was a 'success', the nature of its arcane value system never better revealed than by the anecdote, well known to architects, in which a recently appointed Labour minister of the 1945 government asks the venerable classicist Sir Albert Richardson how much money he requires for research into architecture, only to receive the answer: 'None, architecture is an art.'

Having let the cat out of the bag as regards industry versus profession, with the profession doing all the talking and the nonarchitectural mobile-home industry building all the houses, Davies moves on in the style of Reyner Banham to explore mosts rather than firsts.

He travels to America to explore the mobile-home industry at first hand, and then even more adventurously to Japan to find out how a volume sectional home-builder like Daiwa deals with a market where the house is not so much a credit generator as an expendable consumer product. Davies deals with this diverse material in a masterly fashion, maintaining a pleasingly sceptical tone, an example of which is his frank dismissal of the winner of the 1968 Dupont 'House for Today' competition: 'Nobody remembers who won it, but Richard Rogers came second.'

But where he really scores is in his very well researched account of the Second World War housing programme in the US that produced more than 200,000 prefabricated houses in four years, and not only supplied 12 per cent of the total housing output of the country during that time but also inspired the postwar 'prefab' programmes in the UK and France. Yet, as Davies reminds us, there was failure in the American system too, with the same kind of perfectionism as had blighted the work of Wachsmann and Gropius. But it is the story of the Lustron Home of 1946, also recounted in this book, that should be required reading for every would-be prefabrication tycoon. ⌂

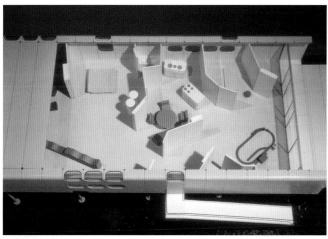

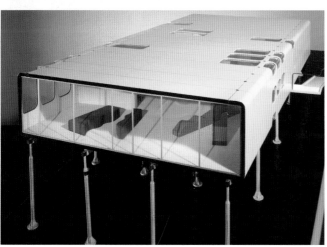

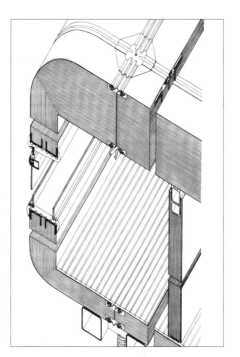

Richard Rogers, Zip-Up, 1968
For Colin Davies, Zip-Up is 'a kind of Yellow Submarine on legs; pink legs. Highly insulated aluminium sandwich panels joined by neoprene gaskets were formed into a structural rectangular tube with rounded corners. It was glazed at the ends and punctured by bus windows, and the space inside could be divided up as the user pleased by mobile partitions locked into position pneumatically. The spindly steel legs were adjustable to accommodate sloping sites. Perhaps harder to build than it looked, it was nevertheless a beautifully simple concept and an appealing image.' It is a generous, extendable and adaptable idea intended to be sold through builders' merchants that may yet serve as a low-density model of Maki's sequential approach to planning.

Prefabricating Memory Lane: Whatever Happened to Systems?

Three decades after his first involvement with an issue of ⟁ on systems buildings, **John McKean**, Professor of Architecture at the University of Brighton, revisits the subject. He concludes that, despite the ensuing years, architects still have much to learn about the mass production of buildings.

Thirty years ago, ⟁ – then a monthly magazine – published a special issue entitled *Whatever Happened to the Systems Approach?* (⟁ May 1976). And I was one of the editorial group who sat around in the ⟁ office talking about whether there was life to be breathed into the thoroughly discredited idea of system building. We had architects intellectualising about industrialised manufacture, standardisation and modularisation. Sets of components and ultra-subtle connectors had been conceptualised ad nauseam. At the same time, we had the big and brutish contractors with their heavy concrete panel systems producing the most god-awful housing environments with the most appallingly shoddy detailing and workmanship on site.

How could systems be rehabilitated? Chaired by Andrew Rabanek, we began by being clear that the subject was not systems as assembled kits of building parts, but systems thinking: dealing with the interaction among components in a complex situation where the whole becomes more than a sum of its bits. The articles looked at how Cedric Price procured work, how Walter Segal minimised superfluous effort, how architects built schools, and what Farrell and Grimshaw saw as their systems approach.

So how would ⟁ think of the term 'systems' today? As a way to procure more and better buildings more quickly? Certainly, we acutely need more dwellings at reasonable cost and close to where people want to work. But the short-termism of more and quicker always leads to disaster when we neglect better.

There is absolutely no reason why systematised, repetitive housing need not provide dense areas of low-key, low-rise, low embodied energy development (as was patchily sketched by the much-loved minimal postwar prefabs). Equally, it could be in vast forms, creating their own urban scale, places comparable for our 21st-century population with the equally vast and audacious, if less democratic, abbeys or palace complexes of old. Back in the 1970s we had all (except for Reyner Banham) lost our nerve over megastructures. And this seemed to imply an equivalent lost nerve in system building generally.

Earlier ideas of great crumbly megastructures had grown from Team X pseudo-organic notions of cluster: from the Smithsons' urban restructuring and Aldo van Eyck's experiments with clustered forms, from Giancarlo De Carlo's (unbuilt) carpets of clustered dwellings,[1] and Jørn Utzon's (built), each with identical units intricately spilled over a landscape. One architect designing a new English university in the early 1960s told me he had poured Lego pieces over the valley of his site model – his attempt to generate a crumbly megastructure. Ideas, mainly from the 'habitat' notions at the centre of Team X, perhaps reached their final megastructural formation in the form literally called 'Habitat', by Moshe Safdie in Montreal, which was completed in 1967. I remember it well, as I tried designing a highly articulated agglomeration of romantically stacked volumetric modules, linked by penthouses cribbed from the Cumbernauld centre, for a high-density housing project as a fourth-year student in 1966.

Megastructural from repetitive volumetric units, perhaps. But not rational systems. In fact, it was the 'system builders' of wall-frame housing, of course, who actually 'renewed' our towns. And so, by the 1970s, architects who mentioned the word 'system' were very defensive indeed.

There were, though, even then, brave attempts at systematising the process of architectural procurement, but these were towards the tail end of a stronger tradition – that of the postwar school, whose story Andrew Saint has told so well.[2] Here was system building that did not have to be megastructural and, by the 1970s – in the days when architects

Giancarlo De Carlo, Team X low-rise clusters of modular units, unbuilt and unpublished project for Matera, Italy, 1953.

Giancarlo De Carlo, Team X low-rise clusters of modular units, unbuilt and unpublished project for Matera, Italy, 1953
The drawings show how the sequence of volumetric units may have been clustered in the landscape.

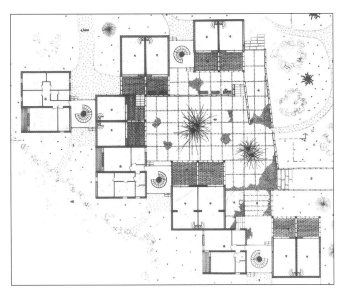

were struck off by the RIBA for even considering getting into bed with a contractor – there was one brave attempt to systematise production. Joined-up building formation, in those distant days when most architects were still acting for their public-sector employer, argued that an architect instructing building workers directly would show a unified organisation that benefited from simplified relationships:

> By making the designer the manager, there is an instant and dynamic dialogue between the design conception of the building and the hard practice of realising it. We still have a lot to learn about building, but of one thing I am certain: connecting design and construction in one single organisation is inherently the most efficient way of building.[3]

That was the conclusion of a fascinating tale by the county architect, Henry Swain, of Nottinghamshire County Council's experiment in systems thinking. I worked with Swain on the article, editing it for the *Architects' Journal*, and I asked Louis Hellman to illustrate it. Hellman himself had been a schools architect, leaving the Inner London Education Authority's architects department at the same time as myself, and for much the same reason. I'd begun a sketch design scheme for a new school that had to be within the straitjacket of the clunky MACE heavy wall panel system and – particularly seeing the charming Edwardian school we had to demolish to make way for it – could bear it no longer. Hellman, more bravely, simply refused to 'design' in MACE. Now, at the *AJ* a few years later, I looked again at the whole business. I was fascinated by the larger system of the building's formation: encouraged by Swain, I enthusiastically read Charles Foster's *Building with Men*.[4] The buzz word was 'holistic' if not yet 'joined-up'.

Though I had previously worked with CLASP, the schools'

system that Nottinghamshire had originated after Hertfordshire County Council's postwar work, this had been on a culturally absurd project. A prestigious public school was exchanging its magnificent, but horrendously inappropriate, Waterhouse-designed building for a loose carpet of post-York University CLASP Mark 4, unfortunately resembling to the inattentive eye nothing so much as the local secondary modern.

CLASP had moved on from its inspiring early transparency: all glass, tile hanging and lightweight steel frame, epitomised in the pavilion that won the Milan Triennale prize in the 1950s. In the 1970s, the inspiration of the Nottinghamshire design/build project was that, on top of the system of bits (CLASP's catalogue of parts) was a real systematic approach to the complete formation – design, procurement and assembly. 'It was started,' Swain concluded, 'because we felt that some of the problems of prefabricated buildings to which we were committed could best be solved if we studied them in a comprehensive way.'[5]

With CLASP it importantly wasn't just more and quicker, but better. Industrial and educational goals could meet in an architecture of spatial subtlety and complexity, where inherent technical problems, like lack of acoustic privacy, was argued by educationalists as a boon rather than a problem, and where, before the 1970s oil crisis, sunlight for children was equated with happiness.

None of this complexity entered the housing system debate. Here, with construction rationalised, but spatial design and quality of experience neglected, the industry-led juggernaut was producing much socially appalling and not a few physically dangerous hutches.

In contrast, our 1976 Δ issue argued, a systematisation of production based on systems thinking at a human scale can

18 *With Ken Wilkinson, an experienced worker, Gunilla Hedman, Christina Johansson and Caroline Robertson— three architectural students from Gothenburg and Edinburgh —assembled steel frame of Arnold Infants School extremely efficiently. It is not easy for women students to get jobs on ordinary building sites for reasons of tradition but they are, of course, just as good as equally inexperienced men students*

encourage an architecture that shows sensitivity towards the user. As the processes of assembly are clarified and demystified, so there comes a transparency not only of production, but of inhabitation. 'With a responsive building,' as Nick Grimshaw said in the same issue, 'clients think more creatively about change' (p 273). What was working for small CLASP primary schools from the 1950s was also working for small Walter Segal timber-frame houses from the 1970s. These buildings could be added to (extra classroom, additional bedrooms) and changed around with ease. Segal, like CLASP (designed for the load-bearing capacity around mine workings), literally touched the earth lightly.

The fundamental difference between the two is that the schools programme had to be large enough to tool up the manufacturers, from Brockhouse's steel frames downwards, to produce the Mecanno sets out of which to build myriad small schools. While for Segal the goal was to avoid creating his own 'specials' at all, to avoid all second forming. So, for example, his grid was based on the size of builders' merchants' standard panels. Economies in process and minimising waste, along with other issues in the formation process, such as just-in-time production and delivery, were central to the systems thinking, and much more than a 'kit of parts'. Segal's bills and specs ensured minimal chaos on site, as they always listed material in the order of its use and thus of delivery and storage.[6] Such an approach, Rabanek said in that *AD* about all those we discussed, was 'driven by crashing common-sense' (p 278).

But there is nothing new in this. Well over a century earlier, Brunel's prefabricated timber hospital for the Crimea was loaded and unloaded and speedily erected in just the same way. Paxton and Fox's Crystal Palace, its module based on the maximum available size of a pane of glass, epitomised the common-sense system. If Paxton's system could unify both rainwater and condensation removal with structure and fire protection, Brunel's system for the Great Western Railway could integrate rail gauge and ticket design, Temple Meads station and the railway timetable.

I have argued in my book on Crystal Palace that its great achievement in 1850 was not so much in technological innovation as in seeing the whole formation of the building as a system.[7] Particularly in the astonishing skills in production engineering that ensured each trade could move steadily through the vast site (it had a footprint the same size as the Millennium Dome) following the one ahead, without ever producing either vast stockpiles (and thus second handling) or chaos. That just-in-time thinking achieved by far the largest glazed building ever, with extraordinarily little wastage in broken glass. The correlation of sources of supply and

Louis Hellman's 1972 view of architectural practice for the *Architects' Journal* feature on Nottinghamshire County Council's Research into Site Management (RSM) initiative. From the *Architects' Journal*, 12 January 1972, p 91.

'Some architects' drawings take longer to prepare and cost more than the actual job on the site.'

'The roles of architect and contractor have been combined . . .'

production held to a revolutionary degree of critical path planning: there was at the centre an exceptional understanding of manufacturing and assembly united in the organisation of labour. 'A response to complexity,' as the editor of *The Buckminster Fuller Reader*,[8] James Meller, described our focus in that 1976 Ⓓ, 'which is characterised by particular emphasis on the whole.'

In the 1970s, in the Nottinghamshire project, as much of the budget went on non-CLASP material as on the CLASP components, to which was added all on-site labour, which became ever more laborious as the buildings approached completion. The well-known Pareto Principle of 80:20 – that, for example, the last 20 per cent of a task takes 80 per cent of the time – can be refined in building production as a parabolic curve as work tends towards 'practical completion'. As Dickon Robinson said to me recently, 'It's that last 5 per cent! All contractors lose interest in the finishing trades.' And

it was to address the issue of the last 5 per cent that Robinson was encouraged to take Peabody into producing housing units with prefabricated completion – first at Murray Grove, and its winning design by Cartwright and Pickard,[9] and then at Raines Court, with Allford Hall Monaghan Morris (AHMM).[10]

The great advantage of prefabricated volumetric units is nothing to do with megastructural forms or constructional systems, but all to do with factory-fitted and finished rooms, sealed until completion. It ensures the quality of that final 5 per cent that is as crucial for occupants as it is for the project's promoter.

Murray Grove was assembled in 10 days on prepared foundations, topped out and watertight, but, as Colin Davies – in his amusing, but immensely instructive book *The Prefabricated Home* – points out, the programme then slipped by 17 weeks, as the decks and balconies, stair and cladding were added.[11] We're back to that CLASP comparison, and what proportion of time/money was spent outside the prefabricated units. With a general contractor, as Robinson points out, it was a five-storey building site. The building inspector demanded scaffolding. Yorkon, or Portakabin rebranded,[12] who produced the units, could probably have assembled them into Peabody's building more cheaply and simply with a routine brick skin. Pickard and Cartwright turned it into solid architecture, Davies adds ironically, while he also maintains that lightweight panels and construction are an affront to architecture's dignity.

Some architects love repetition and order – the Georgian, Classical or Modernist terraced city. Others can't bear its stifling of their egos, and must always have a novel solution to a novel problem. To such architects, the notion of working on housing types – as Walter Segal so subtly developed in his postwar compendium *Home and Environment*[13] – is anathema. The architect's key skill is still in being able to form places, and for them to be of value the systems goals of more and quicker must still be interlinked with, and predicated on, that of better. Ⓓ

Notes

1. John McKean, *Giancarlo De Carlo: Layered Places,* Edition Axel Menges (Stuttgart), 2004.
2. Andrew Saint, *Towards a Social Architecture: The Role of School Building in Post-War England,* Yale University Press (London), 1987.
3. Henry Swain, 'Research into Site Management (RSM)', *Architects' Journal*, 12 January 1972.
4. Charles Foster, *Building with Men*, Tavistock (London), 1969.
5. Henry Swain, op cit.
6. John McKean, *Learning from Segal*, Birkhauser (London), 1989.
7. John McKean, *The Crystal Palace:* London, 1851 by Sir Joseph Paxton and Charles Fox, Phaidon (London), 1994.
8. James Meller (ed), *The Buckminster Fuller Reader*, Jonathan Cape (London), 1970.
9. www.cartwrightpickard.com, accessed 1 August 2005.
10. www.ahmm.co.uk, accessed 1 July 2005.
11. Colin Davies, *The Prefabricated Home*, Reaktion (London), 2005, p 180.
12. www.yorkon.co.uk, accessed 10 August 2005.
13. Walter Segal, *Home and Environment*, Leonard Hill (London), 1953, first published 1948.

Designer Volumetric at IKEA Prices

Volumetric construction is too associated with 'affordable' housing for rent by registered social landlords, or 'microflats' for sale to underpaid 'key workers'. Kisho Kurokawa's Nakagin Capsule Tower, in Tokyo, of 1972, is well known, but it was never intended as a main residence, and provided an extra room in the city. Architects interested in volumetric construction might well be designing gorgeous macroflats and spacious houses, developing the functionality of such buildings, while aiming to bring down costs through repetition. However, **Ian Abley** believes their efforts will continue to be frustrated by the need for site-specific planning approvals, and the cost of developable land in restricted supply.

Kisho Kurokawa, Capsule 'K' Summer House, Nagano, 1973
This project, in Corten steel rather than concrete, as at Nakagin, or stainless steel at Sony, is clustered as a number of rooms around a site-built core.

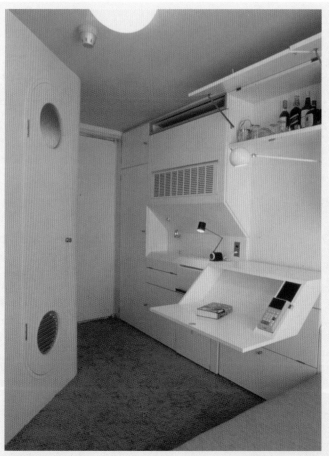

Kisho Kurokawa, Nakagin Capsule Tower, Tokyo, 1972
Kisho Kurokawa in front of the tower in 1972. All the utilities, fittings and appliances for the interior – including the TV – were installed in the factory, an approach that raises the question of design life and upgrade.

These capsule schemes were the culmination of a decade of research by Kurokawa into prefabricated apartments. From 1962 onwards he was thinking about 'master' and 'servant' space, in which the former would have a long design life, as the structural support for the latter, intended to be upgraded over a short timescale. This remains far more sophisticated than the simple stacked boxes built in the UK.

60

Jonathan Schwinge, Over-Sailer, 2005
A speculative 'land-yacht' for the most spectacular landscape, with exceptional deck spaces and views, the clean lines, advanced materials, and serviced self-sufficiency are not inexpensive. This is a made-to-order modular macrohouse with a 394-square-metre (4240-square-foot) interior and 120-square-metre (1292-square-foot) deck, designed for periodic refit around the A-frame structure.

Sybarite Architects, Tree House, 2004
Concept for rural areas, varying from a single-bedroom version up to a five-bedroom model. The approach need not be limited to woodland, being ideal for wetlands and flood plains.

Sybarite Architects, Plectrum, 2005
Proposal for a 40-square-metre (430-square-foot) apartment estimated at £60,000, excluding land and site works, and based on the idea of a permanent core around which units may be upgraded. The Office of the Deputy Prime Minister's 'Design for Manufacture' housing competition required a 76.5-square-metre (823-square-foot) area for that price, but Sybarite aims for a luxury market. In 1975, Kurokawa was looking at a curvilinear three-sided plan around a services core, though on a much larger scale. It may be worthwhile for Sybarite to scale up for mass production of its units.

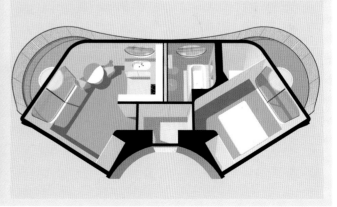

What's Wrong with This Approach, Comrades?

Though strenuously avoiding the 'Modernist' and 'International Style' labels, postwar USSR, along with its Western counterparts, plunged headlong into a system-building programme. Today, Russians know of virtually no other form of housing and, as photographer Bee Flowers observes, the construction sector continues to produce ever larger buildings, for no apparent reason other than habit.

'We must select a smaller number of standard designs ... and conduct our mass building programmes using only these designs over the course of, say, five years ... and if no better designs turn up, then continue in the same way for the next five years. What's wrong with this approach, comrades?' — Nikita Khrushchev, First Secretary of the Soviet Communist Party, 1954

Perhaps it has something to do with anything becoming everything if you look at it for long enough, but after my research in the outer areas of Moscow, I was pleasantly infected with the idea that these public-housing blocks, known as 'microrayons', are underappreciated masterpieces of art. Austere, restrained, never too polished or easy on the eye, they resist classification. However, like a roughly hewn object, like a paint-splattered canvas, they compel through defiant imperfection. Enclosing a central yard, the Soviet microrayon creates a Richard Serra-like monumental space where foreboding walls lurch towards dwarfed pedestrians. Being in the privileged position of the mere spectator who does not have to live there, I am thrilled by that oddly disjointed, disturbed Minimalism.

The microrayon became the basic building block of the residential areas of the socialist city – sets of large buildings in the form of identical blocks. Microrayons are part of a hierarchy of service provision, and several microrayons together form a larger unit for the provision of a wider range of services. Endlessly expandable, without modifications or site-specific considerations, this is the 'generic city' in practice. The Modernist phobia of the street has triumphed: with hardly any facilities for socialisation at street level, people are a scarce sight. Many interiors, too, reveal a striking uniformity in layout, furniture, drapery,

lighting and utensils. The attentive traveller cannot help but wonder what took place here.

Since the 1920s, Soviet architects had laboured on the development of a new form for the city, structurally attuned to the new, socialist lifestyle. Conventional Marxist wisdom dictated that material conditions determine consciousness, making it imperative for these to be altered so as to shape the new collectivist social order. Individual houses were to be replaced with identical living units, thus imposing the uniformity that would cause a substitution of individualism with collectivism. Naturally, the private was swiftly declared political, and petit bourgeois domesticity (which served as a shelter for the tempests of change in society) was to be eradicated in favour of more communal forms of cohabitation. Armed with the slogan 'nothing superfluous', the Communists embarked on the destruction of building interiors that could potentially nurture the old mindset.

However, construction on a large scale in adherence with the principle of 'nothing superfluous' had to wait its turn, as Stalin's anti-intellectual populism gained the upper hand in the early 1930s, and architecture's expressive value was to glorify the freshly rediscovered doctrines of state and nation. But by 1954, Khrushchev denounced Stalin's well-built, thick-walled and ornate buildings as criminally wasteful, and reached back to a mix of utilitarianism and Soviet core values. With efficient construction methods now available, and the country finally sufficiently industrialised to supply materials in large quantities, the face of the USSR's housing stock changed rapidly towards 'honest' and 'rational' boxes, hastily pieced together from concrete slabs.

Domesticity was to wither away along with the state itself, with the target year for such 'full Communism' set at 1988. The newly built houses provided a convenient tabula rasa where reformers could determine the material circumstances of the dwellers. To deal with pre-existing interiors, the state disseminated 'household advice'. In a characteristic wave of planning euphoria, the monofunctional layout of interiors was decried as petit bourgeois. The old space distribution, with furniture arranged along the perimeter of the room focusing on the dining table, was abolished, and the room was divided into functional zones. Such a rearrangement of furniture was designed to break the nucleus of the 'hearth'. The next step was to reduce the number of items of 'material culture' in apartments, towards utopias devoid of objects and commodity fetishism. The dinner table was eliminated, and the dining ritual relegated to the 'mechanical' zone of the kitchen. As far as possible, furniture was made transformable so as to reduce the number of artefacts in the domestic sphere, while simultaneously screening functions deemed inappropriate for the collective room.

Full Communism didn't occur, however, and the envisioned dematerialisation didn't materialise. Today, cities still largely consist of bare-bones concrete boxes and green strips. In a telling scene in a popular Russian movie, a man gets off a plane, drives to his neighbourhood, his street, his building, and turns the key to the front door of his apartment, only to discover later that he's in the wrong city.

Now, with Ikea finally part of the marketplace, Russians have a choice of furniture, but within the monolithic construction industry remarkably little has changed. The sector has no internal stimuli for change, and in the absence of alternatives there are no effective market pressures. Moreover, now that the vast majority of Russians live in system-built housing blocks, these have come to define the urban experience: the expectation of things being any other way has died. Thus, the Russian builder wakes up each morning with the same task as the day before: to build another housing block – a big one. ◌

Functionality rather than Good Intentions in Design

The application of technologies in the field of architecture is devoid of both clarity and leadership, argues **Michelle Addington**, Associate Professor of Architecture at the Harvard School of Design and the author of a new book entitled *Smart Materials and Technologies.*

Academia is saddled with a large knowledge deficit that cannot easily be overcome. Technology is often considered the handmaiden of design and, as such, is meant to be subordinate: design is the why and the what, whereas technology is the how-to. In architecture, technology has traditionally been taught by consultants and/or practitioners in almost an apprentice-type fashion. Students learn technology as a kit of strategies gleaned from what the profession considers good design precedents. Essentially, academia is following practice, not leading it, and this keeps us perennially mired in what we have always done.

Over the last decade, there has been a concerted effort to raise the level of discourse about the role of technology in architecture. Most of today's celebrated design projects attempt to showcase their technology – whether an innovative facade or a 'green' ventilation system – and in doing so also foreground the participating consulting firms. Particular technologies become associated with specific firms, so that the very choice of the consulting team predetermines the technological approach. For example, a design intention for green architecture will probably narrow the field to approximately five major firms, just as a design intention for an expressive structural system will do likewise, although different firms will emerge as the various appropriate consultants.

This does bring some positive benefits. As consulting firms have become more sophisticated there is much greater ability to predict results and, as such, a more established track record. Many more clients are willing to take the risks associated with the adoption of advanced technologies. But the drawbacks may outweigh these benefits. There are fewer 'out-on-a-limb' approaches as each firm refines its definitive contribution. The initial expansion of technologies represented in high-profile projects becomes frozen into a kit of standardised strategies that becomes a powerful model for subsequent applications. And this then cycles back to academia.

Technology courses, woefully light on scientific theory to begin with, are shifting towards survey courses and case studies, all based on existing 'best practice', and thus all serving to further cement in place the existing technological approaches.

There is perhaps an even more profound problem with this encroaching standardisation. As we begin to associate advanced technologies with built projects, we are unable to dis-integrate the various systems: these technologies become so intertwined that one cannot evaluate or examine the impact of any single move. Ironically, even though our design tools and methods have become more sophisticated, we are being forced to resort to empiricism or simulation to investigate technologies – neither experimentation nor theoretical analysis can be applied to these heavily integrated systems. This is highly problematic as legitimate research cannot take place without the underpinning of either experiment or analysis.

Building systems, whether structural, mechanical or environmental, have always been integrated, but more recent technologies have taken this even further. For example, the intention of 'advanced facades' is the collapse of several systems – structural support, cladding, thermal control, ventilation, acoustic control and daylighting – into an *über*-wall that can do everything. A general rule, however, regarding integrated networks is that every additional interconnection increases the complexity of a system by the square. Many other design industries have moved in the opposite direction – searching for the absolute minimum number of components and connections, and we see this represented in the overall trend in development towards tiny and discrete technologies. This puts an unwieldy burden on their transfer into architecture – as technologies developed for direct uses are being appropriated for indirect effects in an infrastructure-laden environment.

Nevertheless, architecture, given that it is neither a

Ultimately, because architecture is read as a construction of effects, our empirical bias leads us to associate certain qualities with certain combinations of technologies. Problematic enough, but when coupled with the changes in architectural theory since the late 1960s that privilege a literary rather than a physical interpretation of effects, our reading of the functionality of technology has become progressively rhetorical.

hierarchical nor clearly bounded enterprise, is not readily amenable to the adoption of a single technology. Whether represented as a room, a building, a complex of buildings, a developed site or an urban area, the architectural project not only comprises the products and knowledge from multiple sources, but each of these products also has an impact on many other systems and domains. As an example, the choice of cladding will alter the energy balance of the surrounding area, and may well have social implications in terms of how a community is represented. The consequences of a new technology are not only limited to the domain in which they were adopted. Does this mean that we are destined to remain wedded to our traditional technological approaches because our problems are so large? Oddly enough, I think that if we become narrower in our problem definition we might be able to bring in smaller and more nimble technologies that will have a much larger impact on our buildings, while giving us much greater control of the consequences.

It all comes down to how we define our problems. The open-ended questions we have in the architecture field aren't readily approached in a discretionary manner. It is not so easy to bracket a problem and define a target: a fundamentally important question such as how to make housing more affordable is not divisible into clearly bounded problems or discrete solutions. When we focus on the small pieces rather than the larger picture, we might be solving the defined problem without addressing the real problem. Indeed, we often cannot draw the line of causation from our solvable problem to the fundamental question.

As an example, the majority of the 2005 budget for research into building systems sponsored by the US Department of Energy was earmarked for projects that increase the air tightness of the building envelope. There is a tacit assumption that the energy use by buildings will decrease if envelopes are tighter and more insulated, even though energy systems are so complex that this direct link does not exist. And herein is a fundamental issue regarding the intention, not the functionality, of a given technology.

Ultimately, because architecture is read as a construction of effects, our empirical bias leads us to associate certain qualities with certain combinations of technologies. Problematic enough, but when coupled with the changes in architectural theory since the late 1960s that privilege a literary rather than a physical interpretation of effects, our reading of the functionality of technology has become progressively rhetorical. Overriding ideologies have assigned value to the intent of technology, not to its functionality. As an example, because some technologies reflect a belief we have in what we deem to be natural, we call those technologies 'green' and assign them with a value – whether energy saving or pollutant reducing – that has no basis in physical law.

There is little disciplinary overview for the technologies that we use in buildings. As a result, we are increasingly saddled with technological systems in architecture that are not only bloated and overintegrated, but which are conceptually inviolate, difficult and indifferent to change. ⧄

Biomimicry versus Humanism

Joe Kaplinsky takes issue with 'biomimcry' and the idea that nature rather than mechanical solutions is the key to unlocking architecture. He argues that biological language and analogies diminish the real achievement of designers. He calls for a humanist sense of what architecture and engineering mean in the world.

Paul Andreu Architecte,
Sea Sphere Maritime Museum, Osaka, 1993–2000

Across the fields of science, engineering, technology and design today there is a flowering of interest in biology. From theoretical physicists studying mathematical models, through chemical engineers devising new products, and architects pushing the cutting edge of design, biology has become a source of ideas and inspiration. Of course, designers of all sorts have always reflected on the natural world. But today the biological inspiration often seems peculiarly isolated from human concerns. Today it seems that the human has become tainted. Synthetic materials are widely reviled as toxic. Design is for 'the planet'.

There is also a positive side to today's interest in biology. In part it is due to the remarkable progress of biological science itself. The most iconic of these advances has been the sequencing of the human genome, but this is only one node in a vast network of advances. The dissemination of insights from biological studies to more distant fields has been aided by the striking and effective use of visual technologies that have spread through biological science, from the graphical presentation of molecular structures through to the biomechanics of locomotion.

Many designers have had their imaginations fired by biological discoveries, which have occurred as new possibilities for the exploration of architectural structures are opening up. Beyond mere presentation tools, the rapid and continuing advance in computer-aided design (CAD) allows the modelling and analysis of engineering and construction in unprecedented ways, while new materials and techniques increasingly stretch the bounds of what is possible. And as Michael Stacey has observed, 'the architect no longer needs to be remote from the manufacturing process; the digital 3-D model can become the building and all of its component parts.'[1] Well, yes, but it is easy to get carried away with the potential. Increasingly, this aspiration, where it exists, is becoming possible, but is far from being commercially commonplace.

Certainly Stacey is right that architects are being positioned to control the generative geometry of their building forms. However, this is still a step or two away from the architect being part of the computer-aided manufacturing (CAM) process that physically forms the building. And let us not forget that the vast majority of buildings are not manufactured, or even prefabricated. As John Thornton of Arup sensibly cautions: 'The danger is that computer power triumphs over design and takes away the need to simplify, rationalise and understand the material. Structural engineers have been concerned for some time that reliance on computers by young engineers can impede the development of their understanding of some aspects of structural behaviour.'[2]

That goes double for CAD-literate architects who might remain strangers to the performance and practicalities of construction. Nevertheless, insights have moved in both directions. Design has informed biology. Claus Mattheck studied how natural structures, and especially trees, distribute stress through structures that bear loads with minimal amounts of material. His computer simulations help create new designs for plates and beams, but also give insight into the way that trees form forks, respond to wind loading and put down roots.[3]

However, there is a problematic side to today's turn towards learning from biology. This is an idolisation of nature that seeks to cut humanity and human achievement down to size. This strand of thought runs through Janine Benyus' *Biomimicry: Innovation Inspired by Nature*, which opens by quoting former president of the Czech Republic Václav Havel: 'We must draw our standards from the natural world. We must honor with the humility of the wise the bounds of that natural world and the mystery which lies beyond them, admitting that there is something in the order of being which evidently exceeds all our confidence.'[4]

Paul Andreu Architecte, Sea Sphere Maritime Museum, Osaka, 1993–2000
The increasing interest in complex curved, and more biological, architectural imagery need not be a retreat from ambitious industrial undertakings.

Frei Otto, Olympic Stadium, Munich, 1972
Naturalistic forms are no less a triumph of human design and productive capacity than mechanistic ones. Image courtesy of Space Imaging

Here we find the key themes of this more environmentally conscious way of thinking, which insists that:

- the natural world places important constraints on our activities
- nature presents mysteries that are beyond our comprehension
- we should be humble and place diminished confidence in our abilities.

These principles stand in direct contradiction to the human-centred outlook associated with the Enlightenment. Principles that have themselves given rise to the achievements of science, technology and engineering on which the positive side of today's nature study is based. It is important to stand up for the positive side of today's interest in biology against the negative. It is also of interest to examine the coexistence of these conflicting forms of thought. So before considering what we can reasonably expect to learn from looking at nature, what are the problems with the three themes of the idolisation of nature?

The first idea, that we should be living within natural limits, breaks down into two common propositions: that we are running up against natural limits, and that by learning from nature we can live within those limits.

This couplet is captured in the common example of energy use. Humanity is condemned for relying on the unsustainable use of fossil fuels. Nature, by contrast, is often idolised as a frugal recycler, breaking down waste and making use of all available resources. If we were to learn from nature, say the biomimics, we would avoid the problems of resource depletion and pollution. But the fossil fuels that supply our energy are, after all, nothing but waste products of nature that escaped its supposedly miraculous recycling process.

The idea that there are natural solutions to natural limits is wrong-headed. Of course we are dependent on nature. However, the way in which we experience such constraints is always mediated by our technological and social systems. It is the comforts of modern technology that allow us to romanticise natural solutions. Without the food security provided by industrialised agriculture there could be no fashion for organic farming. We have lost confidence in human solutions, but not because any 'wisdom' can be found in nature.

The idolisation of natural solutions poses a fundamental challenge not just to a particular style of design, but to the un-natural and social enterprise of designing and building itself. If the goal of sustainable building is to lower impact, and the measure of low impact is untouched nature, then doesn't the ideal logically move towards not building at all?

The second theme, the idea that nature presents us with mysteries beyond our comprehension, also strikes at the very possibility of design. Benyus is rightly intrigued by the study of nature. She sees that 'bees, turtles, and birds navigate without maps, while whales and penguins dive without scuba gear'. Benyus asks: 'How do they do it?' Her list goes on to 'hummingbirds, ants, spiders ... and could be continued indefinitely'.[5]

But would a fish stop to say of a man: 'How does he breathe out of water?' This feat is no less remarkable than any of the others that Benyus lists, yet we do not regard ourselves as

Archigram, Living Pod, 1966
Masters at mixing biological and mechanical imagery, as seen at the retrospective at the Design Museum, London, 2003, while functionality was left unresolved, secondary to the design intent.

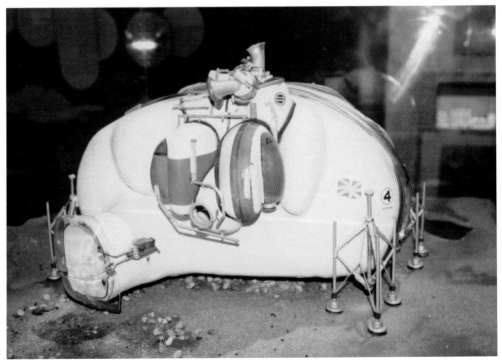

creative by virtue of our capacity to breathe. That is because human ingenuity works as a cultural process quite different to evolution. We say that a scuba suit or an aeroplane are products of creativity because they have consciously been worked on, planned and imagined through application of knowledge about the world. This is a process quite unlike evolution. We should be more impressed with technical achievements than with a fish that has evolved gills.

The third theme of the idolisation of nature is the expectation that we place diminished confidence in human abilities. This is the designer in self-denial, trying to disappear from the mess and effort of having to produce and maintain the built environment by imagining that artifice will turn into a living system. In *Architecture: A Modern View*, Richard Rogers loses sight of the distinction between the human agency of the designer, maker or user of a building, and the fact that architecture is incapable of self-programming for optimal performance: 'Buildings, the city and its citizens will be one inseparable organism sheltered by a perfectly fitting, ever-changing framework. Posts, beams, panels and other structural elements will be replaced by a seamless continuity. These mobile robots will possess many of the characteristics of living systems, interacting and self-regulating, constantly adjusting through electronic and bio-technical self-programming. Man, shelter, food, work, and leisure will be connected and mutually dependent so that an ecological symbiosis will be achieved.'[6]

Life is just not like that. And architecture can never be alive. Nor does nature optimise. At least it rarely optimises what it is that we are interested in. Evolution can only proceed by small steps. It can never start from scratch. Instead, it must optimise incrementally, which can produce some distinctly suboptimal results. For example, no designer would make the nerve connection between the brain and larynx of a giraffe by looping it all the way down the neck and back up to the throat. But evolution was constrained by the anatomy of the giraffe ancestor, in which the nerve looped around a blood vessel at the base of the neck.

Unlike nature, the human imagination can make leaps. It can set to work on a radically new set of design principles. In fact, human innovation is at its most brilliant precisely when it moves beyond incrementalism.

In general terms, living things have evolved under pressure to succeed at reproduction. But the specific consequences of this vary tremendously in different cases. An example is found in the ageing, decay and, ultimately, death of our own bodies. Human biology was shaped by an animal past in which life was nasty, brutish and short. Since the chances of living longer than it took to ensure the survival of offspring was small, there was little pressure to select genes that would allow the body to operate indefinitely. The result is distinctly suboptimal.

Once we understand that the oddities of evolved biology do not necessarily contain the incomprehensible wisdom of the ages, we gain the confidence to appropriate them, and transform them to our own ends. The most striking difference between human technologies and living structures is that whereas human artefacts are manufactured, living things are grown. Related to this, living things are self-sufficient organisms. Our bodies must carry within them not only what

 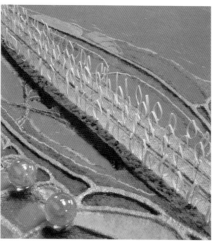 

Eugene Tsui, proposal for Strait of Gibralter floating bridge and island, between Spain and Morocco, 2003
Images show the bridge from Morocco, with a closer view of the floating island and marina. Floating cities are not a new aspiration. 'In the early 1960s I was commissioned by a Japanese patron to design one of my tetrahedronal floating cities for Tokyo Bay,' wrote Buckminster Fuller in *Critical Path* (pp 332–5), two years before his death in 1983. Fuller's floating cities were designed (but sadly never built) for situations ranging from protected harbours through to the deep sea, with increasing use of stabilising underwater pontoons, and with the tetrahedron shape providing a usable sloping-terraced form favoured for the same reasons as in land-based megastructures. That Tsui favours a more organic expression for such an undertaking, while others would prefer a more mechanistic aesthetic, should not obscure the developmental potential of bridging the strait. Unfortunately, it is the mainstream environmentalist critique of industry as an affront to nature that rejects the ambition of environmentally concerned designers like Tsui.

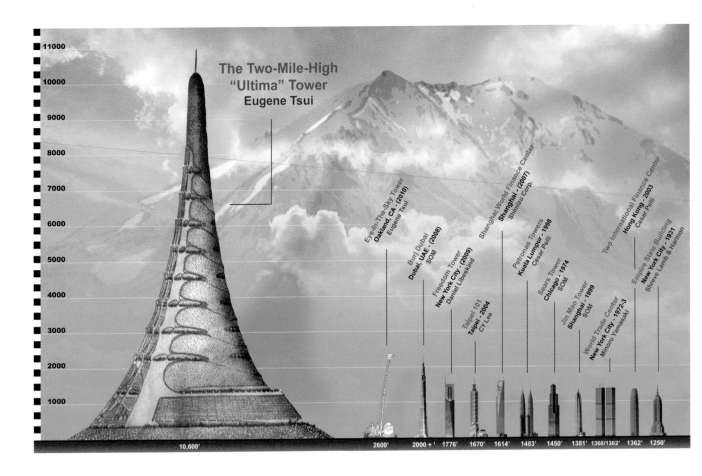

The Two-Mile-High
"Ultima" Tower
Eugene Tsui

11000
10000
9000
8000
7000
6000
5000
4000
3000
2000
1000

Eye-In-The-Sky Tower
Oakland, CA · (2010)
Eugene Tsui

Burj Dubai
Dubai, UAE · (2008)
SOM

Freedom Tower
New York City · (2009)
Daniel Libeskind

Taipei 101
Taipei · 2004
CY Lee

Shanghai World Finance Center
Shanghai · (2007)
Shimizu Corp

Petronas Towers
Kuala Lumpur · 1998
Cesar Pelli

Sears Tower
Chicago · 1974
SOM

Jin Mao Tower
Shanghai · 1999
SOM

World Trade Center
New York City · 1972-3
Minoru Yamasaki

Two International Finance Center
Hong Kong · 2003
Cesar Pelli

Empire State Building
New York City · 1931
Shreve Lamb & Harmon

10,600'   2600'   2000 +'   1776'   1670'   1614'   1483'   1450'   1381'   1368/1362'   1362'   1250'

Eugene Tsui, Ultima Tower, 2005
Inspired by a termite mound, and reminiscent of the organic styles
of Frank Lloyd Wright or his student Bruce Goff, the inhabited surface
is offered as an antidote to urban sprawl. But in contrast, Wright proposed
building upwards and outwards in his Broadacre City, at very low densities
around his needle-like Mile High Illinois of 1956.

'Why build a 2-mile-high [3.2-kilometre] and 1-mile-wide [1.6-kilometre]
city structure?' asks Tsui. 'To stem the onrush of rampant development and
the continued destruction of the natural environment resulting in the
environmental and aesthetic pollution of the Earth,' he answers. But claiming
that 'at current rates, urban sprawl, and its insidious influence, will cover over
and strangle the natural world by the end of this century,' is simply not true.
In any event, his fellow advocates of sustainability would argue that both
ground-level low-density development and mile-high megastructures are part
of the same problem, which they consider to be too many people. Tsui is
unusual in his attempt to develop new forms of human settlement, but his
motivation for doing so encourages his critics – those eco-scaremongers
who doubt the ability of a growing human population to manufacture nature
to our own ends without some cataclysm ending the world as we know it.

is needed for day-to-day functioning, but also for self-repair
and reproduction. In contrast manmade structures like
buildings only make sense when fitted into the complex
network of human society. They must depend on outside
support not just for their construction, but for ongoing
repairs. The simplicity and flexibility that this gives to human
artefacts should not be overlooked.

Manufacture rather than growth opens up new structural
possibilities. But more than this, it allows the innovation of
the factory. If every individual is self-created the available
resources are inevitably limited. The factory and the human
division of labour more generally allow resources to be
concentrated. By making use of the uniquely human capacity
to co-operate, this concentration allows us to achieve a
precision, reproducibility and economy found nowhere in the
natural world.

Freed from the burden of self-repair and reproduction, our
architecture can have a simplicity that is unimaginable in the
living world. It is not only complexity of design that deserves
admiration. Simplicity has its own elegance and economy.
Often it expresses a brilliant insight into the abstract essence
of a problem, discarding irrelevant complications as
unnecessary. The lesson, once again, is that the measure of a
good idea cannot be found in nature alone, but only in how it
is adapted to human ends.

The idea of a building that repairs itself remains an
attractive one, all the more so given the difficulty of realising
it. Today, the idea is often raised in the context of self-
sufficient eco-living, which seems motivated more by the

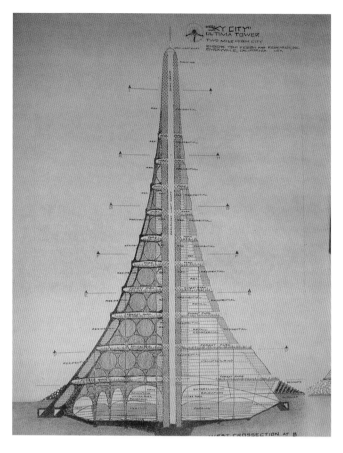

Freed from the burden of self-repair and reproduction, our architecture can have a simplicity that is unimaginable in the living world. It is not only complexity of design that deserves admiration. Simplicity has its own elegance and economy.

notion that society is unreliable or ecologically destructive. There is a difference between a low-maintenance building and an antisocial, autarchic one.

It is at the intersection with ecological design that biomorphic inspiration becomes most problematic. It is here that 'learning from biology' threatens to become little more than an excuse for accommodating ourselves to the natural world as it is, rather than using our creativity to make something new. And amongst the impressive new structures of biomorphic architecture we can detect much idolisation alongside the more positive learning from nature.

In the past, biological references in architecture have tended to be anthropomorphic, as in caryatid columns, or the less conscious influence of the mind's tendency to pick out facial structures in the visual field on a building frontage. Anthropomorphic references have inevitably been closely bound up with human meanings. Think of the complex symbolism of church architecture. The transept and nave are symbolically overlain by the crucified figure, the congregation as the body of Christ, with the priest at its head. Today, biomorphic architecture more reflects the impoverishment of human meanings. The structures of today's buildings refer to animal and plant forms.

Once we recognised that where our cities had become 'concrete jungles', this was symptomatic of our alienation, the breakdown of common values and community. Today's anticipated future skylines recall jungles, too, where wild nature proliferated without rhyme or reason. These new jungles also express a failure to provide meaning. Yet now it

can be celebrated as a turn to nature, outside of human values. The city transformed into jungle is a powerful symbol of a collapsed and lost civilisation, where nature has overgrown the human order.

It is in this dimension of providing significance and meaning to the way in which we understand our buildings that biomimicry is most deficient. We can learn much from nature about chemistry, materials science, and even structural engineering. But we cannot learn how to put together those elements into something greater, or how to become better architects and engineers.

We have much to learn from the study of nature. However, the lesson of history is that as we have learnt more, our transformative impact on the world has grown and not diminished. It is through transforming the world that we have most truly come to understand how it works. In the process we have created a civilisation that has freed us from direct dependence on nature. This freedom has allowed us to appreciate nature aesthetically and scientifically. ∆

Notes
1. Michael Stacey, 'In my craft and sullen art, or Sketching the future by drawing on the past', ∆ *Design Through Making*, July/August 2005, p 42.
2. John Thornton, 'Fabrication research', ibid, p 103.
3. Claus Mattheck, *Design in Nature: Learning from Trees*, Springer Verlag (Berlin) 1998, originally published in German, 1997.
4. Janine M Benyus, *Biomimicry: Innovation Inspired by Nature*, Perenial (New York), 2002, p 1, first published William Morrow, 1997.
5. Ibid, p 6.
6. Richard Rogers, *Architecture: A Modern View*, Thames and Hudson (London), 1990, p 60.

Our Overdeveloped Sense of Vulnerability

Industrialised development and the suburban megalopolis are commonly regarded as a threat to nature, contributing to the increasing frailty of the planet and its delicate ecosystems. Here, Frank Furedi, Professor of Sociology at the University of Kent, looks beyond the immediate environmental factors and assesses the root causes of our ensuing sense of vulnerability, as our worldview is increasingly informed by a collapse in social self-confidence.

The vast scale of the built environment often invites a dystopian response. The megacity frequently provokes a hostile reaction from the anti-Modernist imagination. In the early 20th century, Oswald Spengler associated the decline of Western civilisation with the rise of the city. He believed that human creativity expanded the gap between people and nature. The very attempt to control nature through the application of technology was a 'monstrous' idea as 'old as the Faustian culture itself'.[1] Pessimistic cultural commentators echoed Spengler's lament and portrayed the construction of large cities as an act of human self-destruction. It was in this vein that Lewis Mumford wrote, in his *The Culture of Cities* of 1938, of the trend towards the implosion of the urban environment.[2] Nevertheless, such pessimistic accounts failed to capture the popular imagination. Historically, the scale of the built environment inspired in people a sense of awe. The excitement and stimulation of the big city ensured that urbanisation was culturally affirmed in most industrial societies.

In recent decades the growth of what I characterised as a culture of fear has led to a reorientation in how megacities are perceived.[3] Throughout the 19th and 20th centuries perceptions of the city as resilient competed with perceptions that stressed its vulnerability. In recent times, issues associated with megacities tend to be framed through the paradigm of vulnerability.[4] This approach is strikingly illustrated in a recently published report: *Megacities – Megarisks*. The authors of this report claim that the very size of megacities makes them vulnerable. It is stated that they are 'practically predestined for risks', and are 'more vulnerable than rural areas'.[5] The report uses the term 'vulnerable' as a metaphor to describe the state of existence of the megacity.

THINK! Team, proposal for World Cultural Center, New York, 2002–03
This wonderful megastructural runner-up in the competition to redevelop Ground Zero, argued critic Herbert Muschamp, should have won, but was unfortunately pipped to the post by Daniel Libeskind's 'memorial'. The THINK! Team was Shigeru Ban Architects, Frederic Schwartz Architects, Ken Smith Landscape Architect and Rafael Viñoly Architects.

With vulnerability as its defining condition, the megacity is transformed into a territory that lacks the capacity for resilience. An important influence on the framing of the vulnerability of the megacity is the reversal of the Modernist conceptualisation of the relationship between technology and nature. From the Modernist perspective, science, technology and design protected humanity from the threat of nature. Increasingly today, technology does not so much protect as create the problems – large urban agglomerations being one of them.

The burning twin towers of the World Trade Center, New York, and a satellite image of Ground Zero, cleared after the destruction of the towers on 11 September 2001. Satellite image courtesy of Space Imaging

Western societies have become deeply estranged from the legacy of modernity. During the past four decades, modernisation has tended to be experienced as a destructive and frightening force. According to the cultural critic Marshall Berman, for many people modernisation appears as a 'disastrous mistake, an act of cosmic hubris and evil'.[6] In previous times people fled to the city for protection. But now the anti-Modernist imagination saw the city not as a site for gaining security, but as dangerous and risky territory. The anxieties transmitted by publications such as *Megacities* are not based on new empirical evidence regarding hitherto-unknown dangers of the urban environment. Such anxieties about the built environment are the product of cultural attitudes towards the ideal of resilience and of vulnerability. Contemporary culture possesses a heightened sense of vulnerability and, as a result, tends to transmit a sense of anxiety towards buildings and the urban environment.

One reason for this development is the emergence of safety as an important cultural value in itself. Since the 1970s the question of 'How safe is safe enough?' tends to be met with the answer 'We do not know!' This fundamental reconceptualisation of safety is directly linked to the growing perception that humans are far more vulnerable than it was hitherto believed. The Modernist risk-taking and experimentative imagination that prevailed throughout most of the 20th century had become modified by the rise of an expansive mood of vulnerability.

As a dimension of cultural discourse, the concept of vulnerability emerged in the 1970s and was promoted by the environmentalist movement. It was central to a new narrative that regarded the question of safety from an ecological perspective. According to this orientation, societies and communities are always vulnerable to disasters and acts of violent disruption. From the standpoint of this new vulnerability paradigm, disasters are a normal feature of societies who are unable to deal with the hazards they confront.

'Above all, then, disasters are considered to be primarily about processes in which hazardous events represent moments of catharsis along a continuum whose origins lie buried in the past and whose outcomes extend into the future,' writes Gregory Bankoff in *Rendering the World Unsafe*.[7] Many environmentalists regard the attempt by humanity to manipulate nature as a misguided attempt to dominate forces that are beyond control. The promoters of the ecological concept of vulnerability are critical of a stance that presumes to control nature. They insist that communities are likely to prove too vulnerable when confronted with the more powerful forces of nature.

It is important to note that the concept of vulnerability did not emerge from the experience of adversity confronting communities. It is a term of description or a form of diagnosis that professionals adopt in their characterisation of communities. Even advocates of this concept concede that this is a term that outsiders use to label others. As Annelies Heijmans noted, vulnerability is not a 'concept that grassroots communities use'. She believes that 'vulnerability to disasters is a matter of perception', and 'the view of local people is lacking'. Heijmans adds that 'most agencies tend to think on behalf of the victims, not realizing that disaster-prone communities might interpret their circumstances differently'.[8] Some proponents of the vulnerability paradigm recognise that the concept 'encourages a sense of societies and people as weak, passive and pathetic'.[9]

It is worth noting that contrary to the views advanced through the vulnerability paradigm, communities – even those living in shanty towns in Mexico City or Nairobi – engage with their circumstances as problem solvers. When faced with hazards, communities usually demonstrate a capacity to cope with them. This is why the local communities that are diagnosed as vulnerable by aid agencies have 'no concept of "vulnerability"'. Indeed, in 'local dialects, there is seldom an appropriate translation for the term'.[10] It is also important to recall that large urban centres that have faced devastation through disaster – from the Lisbon earthquake of 1755 to that in Kobe in 1995 and, of course, New York 9/11 in 2001 – have demonstrated a capacity to adapt, improvise and overcome adversity.

The vulnerability paradigm has emerged from a Western cultural imagination that regards the world as a more and more out of control and dangerous place. This perspective is informed by a perception that regards human society as paying a price for its apparent irresponsible behaviour to the environment. One of its principal claims is that disasters are dramatically increasing in number and that human communities have become more and more vulnerable to their impact. 'People are more vulnerable to disasters than in the past,' commented Peter Walker, Head of the Disaster Policy Department at the International Federation of Red Cross and Red Crescent Societies.[11] The message conveyed by this statement is that the cumulative impact of human irresponsibility towards the environment has led to the creation of a new era of catastrophes. The insistence on the growth of human vulnerability is motivated by an ideological estrangement from modernity.

The modern world is experienced as a vulnerable one. 'Basically, the increase in number and severity of natural and technological disasters constitutes one of the clearest tests available of the lack of resilience and sustainability of many human environmental adaptations', notes the author of a review on anthropological research on disasters.[12] As a growing range of human experiences are associated with disasters, the distinction between normal daily life and a disaster becomes ill-defined. The concept of vulnerability helps normalise anxiety towards change, be it social or technological. From this perspective, disaster ceases to possess any distinct features. It is but an extreme symptom of a general state of vulnerability.

The paradigm of community and individual vulnerability provides the dominant cultural conceptual framework for making sense of public anxiety towards innovation and life in an urban setting. Vulnerability is not a state of being that emerges in response to an act of misfortune – it is something that precedes it. It is conceptualised as the 'intrinsic predisposition to be affected, or to be susceptible to damage'.[13] This is why, in recent times, it has become common to use the recently constructed concept of vulnerable groups.

Vulnerable groups does not simply refer to a small minority of economically insecure individuals. Children, indeed all children, are automatically assumed to be vulnerable. A study of the emergence of the concept of vulnerable children shows that in most published literature, the concept is treated 'as a relatively self-evident concomitant of childhood which requires little formal exposition'. It is a taken-for-granted idea that is rarely elaborated and 'children are considered vulnerable as individuals by definition, through both their physical and other perceived immaturities'. Moreover, this state of vulnerability is presented as an intrinsic attribute. It is 'considered to be an essential property of individuals, as something which is intrinsic to children's identities and personhoods, and which is recognisable through their beliefs and actions, or indeed through just their appearance'.[14] Women, the elderly, the poor and the disabled are also represented as vulnerable.

On 26 December 2003, a powerful earthquake struck southeastern Iran, killing more than 43,000 people, injuring 20,000 and leaving 60,000 homeless. It destroyed about 60 per cent of the city of Bam. The old quarter and the 2000-year-old citadel, severely damaged by the earthquake, were built primarily of mud brick. The oldest type of modular megastructure, Bam was still inhabited when it should have been abandoned for better-engineered 21st-century development, leaving it as a tourist attraction or an archaeological site. Image courtesy of Space Imaging

Frank Furedi's latest book is the *Politics of Fear: Beyond Left and Right* (London, Continuum, 2005).

This way of understanding people informs mainstream studies of disaster. One research project exploring the 1998 floods in England recruited participants for its focus groups from what it characterises as 'particularly vulnerable populations who were likely to experience more severe impacts; these included the elderly, single parents, ethnic minority groups, and those of lower economic status'.[15] From this perspective, vulnerability is a key marker and defining feature of a wide variety of group identities.

The ascendancy of the vulnerability paradigm is strikingly evident in changing attitudes towards children. Until the 1970s, the literature tended to associate the response of children to adversity with their capacity for resilience, especially if their families were able to serve as sources of social support. 'But about the middle of the 1970s the tone began to change as researchers began to scrutinize the matter more carefully,' notes Thomas Drabek.[16] The main consequence of this new focus on children's mental health was to call into question the power of children's resilience. According to Frankenberg, Robinson and Delahooke, writing in 2000, the tendency to frame children's problems through vulnerability is a relatively recent development. Their search of a major bibliographical database (BIDS) revealed more than 800 refereed papers between 1986 and 1998 that focused on the relationship between vulnerability and children. They noted that 'whilst in the first four years of this period there were under 10 references each year to vulnerability and children, an exponential increase to well over 150 papers a year occurred from 1990 onwards'. They believe that this figure underestimates the tendency to interpret children's lives through the prism of vulnerability since it ignores the substantial nonacademic literature on the subject.[17]

The association of vulnerability with childhood indicates how the ideal of resilience has lost its salience for everyday cultural life. Resilience is still used as a term that signifies a counterpoint to vulnerability. But invariably it is used as a second-order concept that implies that resilience is a counter-trend to the dominant state of vulnerability. This point is rarely made explicit, but in most of the discussion around problems such as disasters or the threat of terrorism, vulnerability is perceived as the norm and resilience is presented as a potential counter-trend against it. The term 'resilience' tends to be used in a way that presupposes the primacy of vulnerability – resilience is the exception, the modifying factor – rather than the defining state. It is often represented as the counterpoint to a risk factor. Resilience is seen as a protective factor that limits the negative impact of adversity on the individual. It is represented as primarily an antidote to a prior and more fundamental fact of life. From this standpoint, the state of vulnerability is logically prior to the process of resilience.

Reversing this relationship constitutes the principal challenge to those who embrace the cause of human progress. ⚙

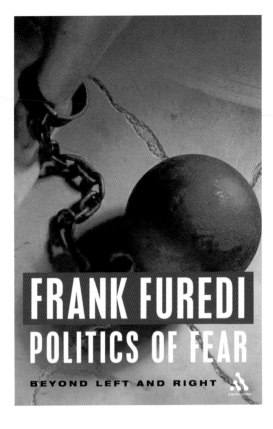

Notes
1. Oswald Spengler, *Man and Technics: A Contribution to a Philosophy of Life*, George Allen and Unwin (London), 1932, p 84.
2. Lewis Mumford, *The Culture of Cities*, Harcourt Brace and Co (New York), 1938.
3. Frank Furedi, *The Culture of Fear: Risk Taking and the Morality of Low Expectations*, Continuum Press (London), 2005.
4. Frank Furedi, *Therapy Culture: Cultivating Vulnerability in an Uncertain Age*, Routledge (London), 2004.
5. Munich Re Group, *Megacities – Megarisks: Trends and Challenges f or Insurance and Risk Management*, Munich Re (Munich), 2005, pp 4 & 18.
6. Marshall Berman, *All That Is Solid Melts Into Air: The Experience of Modernity*, Verso (London), 1995, p 82.
7. Gregory Bankoff, 'Rendering the world unsafe: "vulnerability" as Western discourse', *Disasters*, Vol 25, No 1, 2001, p 30.
8. Annelies Heijmans, 'Vulnerability: A Matter of Perception', paper given at the International Work conference on 'Vulnerability in Disaster Theory and Practice' organised by Wagenningen Disaster Studies, 29–30 June 2001, p 1 & 15.
9. Bankoff, op cit, p 29.

10. Heijmans, 'op cit, p 4.
11. Peter Walker, 'There are no natural disasters', *Geographical*, July 1994.
12. A Oliver-Smith, 'Anthropologicald research on hazards and disasters', *Annual Review of Anthropology*, Vol 25. 1996, p 304.
13. M Cardona, 'The need for rethinking the concepts of vulnerability and risk from a holistic perspective: A necessary review and criticism for effective risk management', in G Bankoff, G Frerks and D Hilhorst (eds), *Mapping Vulnerability: Disasters, Development and People*, Earthscan Publishers (London), 2001, p 2.
14. R Frankenberg, I Robinson and A Delahooke, 'Countering essentialism in behavioural social science: The example of the "vulnerable child" ethnographically examined', *The Sociological Review*, 2000, pp 588–89.
15. Sue Tapsell, 'The health effects of floods: The Easter 1998 floods in England', *Flood Hazard Research Centre Article Series*, No 3/99, FHRC, p 2.
16. Thomas E Drabek, *Human System Responses to Disaster: An Inventory of Sociological Findings*, Springer-Verlag (New York), 1986, p 271.
17. Frankenberg, Robinson and Delahooke, op cit, p 587.

Eero Saarinen and the Manufacturing Model

Jayne Merkel, board member of ⚟ and the author of an authoratitive new book on Eero Saarinen, describes how Saarinen did much to advance the design of mass-producible architecture in an era of postwar optimism. She traces both the roots of Saarinen's approach and describes how it sits alongside his carefully crafted expressionistic work, such as the TWA Terminal at JFK.

It may have been Walter Gropius and his Bauhaus colleagues who promoted the idea of manufactured architecture, but it was Eero Saarinen who actually made some inroads into it. While Gropius developed an industrial aesthetic for the Bauhaus at Dessau, and emphasised mass production in its curriculum (a significant departure from Henry van der Velde's Arts and Crafts earlier approach at Weimar), Saarinen actually designed manufacturable buildings, created mass-produced furniture, developed new architectural materials, and used techniques from manufacturing in building and design to a much greater extent than any of the Bauhaus masters did. Almost certainly, he would have pulled the disparate threads of these innovations together to advance mass-producable architecture if he had not died suddenly in 1961 in what should have been the middle of his career, while

the John Deere headquarters, Dulles Airport, and half a dozen of his other major buildings were still under construction.

Eero Saarinen's best-known works – the TWA Terminal, St Louis Gateway Arch, the Yale Ice Hockey Rink – are anything but modular and manufacturable. They are experimental, expressionistic, one-of-a-kind creations that required enormous technological skill and infinite patience to build. But Saarinen always pursued several directions at once, and from the time he was a boy one of them always seemed to be an interest in mass production.

The son of the Finnish early-Modern architect Eliel Saarinen, he was taught that it was important to be 'a man of his time' and encouraged to develop a voice of his own. As a child in Finland, he spent his days drawing at the big table in his father's home studio while Eliel and his colleagues were

Eero Saarinen and Associates with Ammann & Whitney Engineers, Dulles Airport, Chantilly, Virginia, 1958–63.

Eero Saarinen and Ralph Rapson, Demountable Space Community House for the United States Gypsum Company, 1940
This project was designed to show potential uses for gypsum board as a building material that could make spaces that could be used for temporary purposes and altered to fit various needs.

Charles Eames (left) and Eero Saarinen at Cranbrook Academy, demonstrating the strength of a high-tensile structure they created to display student work for an exhibition in 1939.

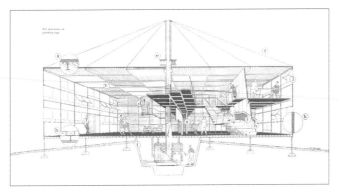

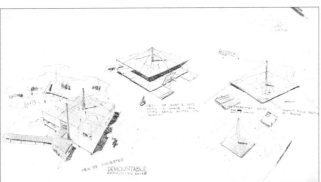

designing everything from city plans to silverware, and his mother, Loja, was making architectural models and doing her own art work.

In America, to which the Saarinens emigrated in 1923 when Eero was 12, Eliel was invited by the newspaper magnate George Gough Booth to design the schools and museums that would become the Cranbrook Educational Community outside Detroit. The whole family was involved in their design. Loja made Eliel's models and fabrics in the weaving studios she established there. Eero's sister Pipsan developed decorative motifs and colour schemes for the interiors. And at just 15 years old, Eero created sculptural reliefs and metalwork details for the Cranbrook School for Boys. When he was 18, he designed the master bedroom of the house his parents built at Cranbrook, and in the next two years (1929–30) while in high school and spending a year in Paris studying sculpture, he designed light fixtures, stained-glass windows, and chairs for the Kingswood School for Girls.

Most of these blended rather seamlessly into the carefully crafted, Wrightian, brick-and-copper Kingswood buildings, though his bent-birch dining hall chairs resemble similar ones that Saarinen family friend Alvar Aalto created for the Viipuri Library (1931–3). But the tubular steel chairs that Eero designed for the Kingswood auditorium were of an entirely different order – more like those Marcel Breuer and Mies van der Rohe were working on at the Bauhaus (1926–30). They were not only intended to be mass-produced, but also had an industrial aesthetic that is almost antithetical to his father's approach. Cranbrook, after all, was founded as an Arts and

Eero Saarinen, Unfolding House, 1942
This project, composed of modular trailer units, was shippable and
expandable as its metal-skin roof could stretch over a larger area.

Crafts community, but Eliel was an unusually open-minded
and progressive teacher who encouraged his students (and his
son) to pave their own ways.

The tubular-steel chairs were done even before Eero left
home in 1931, to study architecture at the then Beaux Arts
Yale University School of Architecture, and to spend two years
in Europe on a travelling fellowship, where he could examine
the work of the European avant-garde at first hand. When he
returned in 1936, the Cranbrook Academy of Art was in full
swing, his father was president, teaching on the
apprenticeship model, and an incredibly talented group of
young people were experimenting with various media. There
was a beautiful gifted sculptor Lily Swann, who became his
first wife. There was Florence Schust, a girl his parents had
befriended when she was a student at Kingswood, who went
on to study architecture, marry a furniture-maker named
Hans Knoll and create Knoll International. Harry Bertoia, who
later produced sculptural decorations for many of Eero's
buildings, was there studying sculpture and design, as were
the architects Ralph Rapson and Harry Weese, and the all-
purpose designers Charles and Ray Eames, who met and
married at Cranbrook.

'Charlie' Eames became Eero's best friend as well as a
frequent collaborator. Though he had worked as a traditional
architect before he came to Cranbrook, under Eliel's influence
he branched out. Although Eero was practising with his father
and teaching at the academy, he and Charlie designed a light
tensile structure to support work shown in a Cranbrook
student exhibition in 1939. The next year, with other
Cranbrook students, they entered the Museum of Modern
Art's 'Organic Design in Home Furnishings' competition and
won first prizes both for modular wooden cabinets, similar to
the metal ones Breuer had created at the Bauhaus, and for
double-curved chairs with plywood shells, foam-rubber
padding and upholstery, rather like Alvar Aalto's bent
plywood ones, but softer and more playfully free form. The
storage units and chairs were manufactured, but they were
not mass-produced and marketed because of the onset of the
Second World War. However, both architects' interests in
furniture were encouraged, and Eero went on to create a
series of popular chairs and tables with Florence Schust (later
'Shu' Knoll Bassett) for Knoll.[1] Among the most popular were
those in the white plastic Pedestal (Tulip) series that combined
his interests in sculpture and mass production.

Always interested in all scales, Eero also developed, with
Ralph Rapson, a so-called 'Demountable Space' for the United
States Gypsum Company, which had hired them in 1940 to
devise new uses for their products. It had a tensile roof hung
from a central mast similar to that on Buckminster Fuller's
Dymaxion House (1927–30), and could be reconfigured or
expanded in modular units, as its plumbing and heating pipes
were contained in prefabricated cores.

In 1941, Saarinen proposed the 'Unfolding House' composed

of modular trailer units that could be shipped to a site and
arranged in various combinations. It had a shimmering, gently
curved metallic roof that could unroll to cover additional areas
and a prestressed metal skin similar to the surface he later
used on the St Louis Gateway Arch.

During the Second World War, the family firm, Saarinen,
Swanson and Saarinen (J Robert Swanson was married to
Eero's sister), designed several communities for defence
plants. The one in Center Line, Michigan, for Kramer Homes
(1941–2) was composed of attached one- and two-storey
houses, with flat or gabled roofs, arranged around a central
open space with a school, park, playgrounds and restricted
vehicular access. And since the 477 efficient, one- to three-
bedroom units had to be built quickly and cheaply (for an
average of $3075), Eero was able to experiment with
prefabrication and modular construction to some extent.

The innovative editor of *California Arts & Architecture*
(later *Arts & Architecture*) magazine, John Entenza, also
provided opportunities to explore modularisation. In 1943,
the magazine held a 'Designs for Postwar Living' housing
competition underwritten by manufacturers of building
materials. Eero entered with Oliver Lundquist, and their
design for flat-roofed, glass-walled housing units, with
packaged service cores that could be variously combined, won
first prize. The pre-assembled components (PACS) came in two
configurations – a kitchen, bedroom and bath, or a bedroom
and bath. The architects said they could be attached to living
spaces in detached houses, terrace houses, motels or even
tents. They argued: 'The economic and social demands for
postwar housing must be met by extensive utilization of our
assembly-line potential.' They even optimistically 'estimated
that PAC can answer 80 percent of postwar housing demands'.[2]

Two years later, in 1945, Eero designed two of the magazine's
famous Case Study Houses with Charles Eames, for adjacent

Eero Saarinen with Robert Swanson, Defense Houses for Kramer Homes, Center Line, Michigan, 1941–2
These houses for defence workers were made of frame construction, one and two storeys high, and combined in rows for two to eight families, with both pitched and flat roofs. Service areas and kitchens face driveways; formal entrances face walkways in the progressive plan which separated traffic from pedestrians.

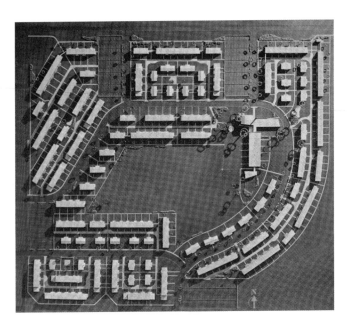

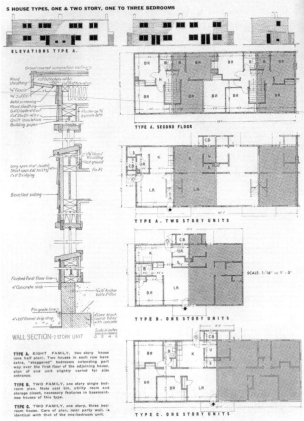

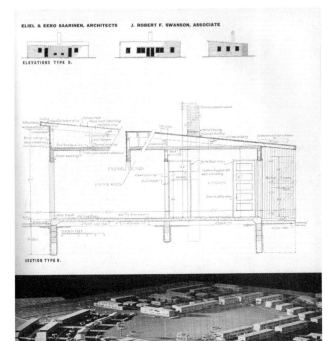

sites in Pacific Palisades (a Los Angles suburb) overlooking the Pacific Ocean. One of them, Number 8, intended for the Eames, was later altered, but the other, Number 9, for Entenza himself, was built according to the plans. The two houses, both made of mass-produced materials – steel, glass, ferroboard – were almost opposites. The Eames House was long and narrow, and straddled a hilly site like a bridge. Entenza's was square and ground-hugging: it had a pinwheel plan and a terrace continuous with the main living space.

When they built their house, the Eames rotated it, placing the short end towards the ocean, moved it to the edge of the site on to flatter ground, and filled in the ground floor. But they left the structural frame exposed. It is concealed in the Entenza House, so the manufactured parts are not as visible.

The year before the houses were designed, in 1944, Saarinen, Swanson and Saarinen received a commission from General Motors that would enable Eero to explore mass production on a massive scale. But he was still in Washington DC, serving in the Office of Strategic Services (the predecessor of the Central Intelligence Agency) on war duty designing reports, and the first scheme the firm developed was not very radical. Fortunately, building was postponed for several years and by the time it began, in 1948, the original Art Moderne scheme was over budget. Also, by that time, Eero had won the competition for the St Louis Gateway Arch (which his father had entered separately) and had begun to assume leadership of the firm.

Eero's General Motors Technical Center (1948–56) was made of manmade materials (shiny metal, coloured baked enamel panels, glass) similar to those used for automobiles. Although it was strongly influenced by the campus that Mies van der Rohe was building in Chicago for the Illinois Institute of Technology at the time (Eero made frequent trips to see Mies and his work there), GM is many times larger – 130 hectares (320 acres)

Eero Saarinen and Associates, General Motors Technical Center,
Warren, Michigan, 1948–56
The ceiling grid in the studios and drafting rooms contained electrical outlets, air-conditioning ducts, sprinkler heads and diffusers for different lighting effects, and was coordinated with the structural grid so that wall panels could be moved anywhere within the module.

Eero Saarinen and Associates, IBM manufacturing facility, Rochester, Minnesota, 1956–8
Aerial view showing expandable chequerboard plan. The long, narrow blocks are composed of two storeys of offices; the big square ones contain tall single-storey manufacturing areas.

instead of 16 hectares (40 acres) – and on an automobile, rather than a pedestrian, scale. However, its curtain walls are built on a manufacturable 1.5-metre (5-foot) module, instead of Mies's more architecturally scaled 7-metre (24-foot) one, and they conceal, rather than express, the structural frame.

The GM Technical Center grew into a $100-million project, with $60 million for the 25 buildings alone. The buildings are arranged at right angles around a 9-hectare (22-acre) rectangular lake and set off by a soaring water tower and hemispherical dome, both sheathed in reflective stainless steel.

The buildings not only look like manufactured objects, they were designed and built like them. Saarinen and his colleagues had at their disposal the resources of the GM engineering and design staffs who taught them to work with full-scale models the way automobile designers do, and helped them develop what Eero called many 'firsts'.

'We had previously used a baked enamel-finished panel on the pharmacy building at Drake University, which may well have been the very first instance of the now so familiar metal curtain wall. But General Motors represents the first significant installation of laminated panels and the first use anywhere of a uniquely thin [2.5-inch-/6.4-centimetre-thick] porcelain-faced sandwich panel' – a completely prefabricated exterior and interior wall. 'For the project we also developed the brilliantly colored glazed brick' on the ends of the buildings. 'Perhaps the greatest gift to the building industry is the development of the neoprene gasket weather seal', similar to those used in windscreens, 'which holds fixed glass and porcelain enamel metal panels to their aluminum frames. It is truly windproof and waterproof and is capable of allowing the

glass or panels to be "zipped" whenever a building's use changes. All of these developments have become part of the building industry and a common part of the language of modern architecture,' Eero explained.[3]

The ceilings in the drafting rooms are the first completely modular luminous ceilings. Their flexible plastic pans can be tilted to provide various lighting effects, and they incorporate the air-conditioning system, electrical outlets and sprinkler heads. The ceiling grid itself is coordinated with the structural grid. It contains anchor posts for the movable partition system, so the partitions can always be aligned with the ceiling grid, and the ceiling system works in any plan configuration. This modular, multisystem device made possible the completely controlled 'manufactured' environment that became the norm for American corporate offices.

The GM Technical Center commission led to other corporate campuses where Saarinen and his colleagues, especially John Dinkeloo, developed new manmade materials and mass-producible construction techniques. Rarely did Saarinen start out with any particular objective. The approach he took always grew out of research undertaken for the task at hand. For an IBM manufacturing and engineering facility in Rochester, Minnesota (1956–8), he and his colleagues not only created even thinner, more efficient wall panels than those at GM, but also developed a modular plan for future expansion using the same kind of plus-and-minus logic as early computers. Employing a ratio IBM had developed, the architects created a 5574-square-metre (60,000-square-foot) single-storey module for the factory spaces and a 3716-square-metre (40,000-square-foot) two-storey one for offices,

**Eero Saarinen and Associates with Ammann & Whitney Engineers,
Mobile Lounge, Dulles Airport, Chantilly, Virginia, 1958–63**
Overall view of mobile lounge connecting to an aeroplane.

engineering labs and classrooms, and built the whole complex out of them—around courtyards in a chequerboard pattern that could be expanded in a rational, orderly way as needed. Wall panels and office plans were based on a 1.2-metre (4-foot) module (even smaller than that at GM), and the window bands were set at the same height throughout, so the whole seems more uniform – and more manufactured – than at GM.

The Thomas J Watson Research Center, which Saarinen also designed for IBM, in Yorktown, New York (1957–61), is freer in form since the building curves around the crest of a hill. And the use of rough stone makes it appear part of the rugged landscape. But the plans of the laboratories – designed concurrently with those for Bell Telephone Laboratories in Holmdel, New Jersey, and employing the same system – are modular, with laboratories back-to-back on one side of a corridor and scientists' offices back-to-back along the other side across from their laboratories. Saarinen used new kinds of reflective glass in both buildings, fully mirrored for the first time in Holmdel. For the John Deere Company Headquarters in Moline, Illinois (1957–64), Saarinen and Dinkeloo developed self-rusting Corten steel into an architectural material and used it boldly for the exposed structural frame, bridges between sections and for bold exterior sunscreens.

However, it was at Dulles Airport, outside Washington DC (1958–63), that he took the idea of modularity to a logical conclusion. Not only was the 183-metre (600-foot) long concourse designed to be expanded by another 91 metres (300 feet) on each side, as indeed it was in 1996, but the building was made with movable parts. To avoid the long corridors passengers already had to travel to get to their planes at the

time, the architects created 'mobile lounges' – movable waiting rooms – to take them there instead. These lounges were, of course, produced in factories, and though flimsier versions have been added over the years they are still in use, though now they usually take passengers to satellite concourses instead of to the planes themselves. The thinking that went into them, the logic of an industrial designer or engineer, was almost antithetical to that behind Saarinen's other great airport, the TWA Terminal at John F Kennedy Airport in New York, which is the work of a sculptor modelling on an architectural scale. But to Eero Saarinen, art and science, industry and objecthood were all part of a single thing he called 'architecture'. ∆

Notes
1. See 'American Moderns: Eero Saarinen and His Circle', *Architectural Design*, July 2002, pp 26–33.
2. 'Prize Winners in California Arts and Architecture's Designs for Postwar Living Competition', *The Architectural Forum*, September 1943, p 89.
3. Aline Saarinen (ed), *Eero Saarinen on His Work*, Yale University Press (London and New Haven), 1962, p 32.

Jayne Merkel is the author of *Eero Saarinen* (Phaidon Press), 2005, hb £45 (US$75.00). This is the definitive monograph of the life and work of Eero Saarinen, which in a highly readable text brings together original research alongside fascinating archive photographs and drawings.

Think Big for the Developing World

2005 was tagged the 'year of Africa'. In fact, it should go down in history as the year Africa's development was firmly reined in by Western policy-makers, say Ceri Dingle and Viv Regan, director and assistant director of the education charity, NGO and NVYO WORLDwrite. Africa needs development, but not the small-minded sustainable variety. Could it be that a lack of confidence and ambition in development among the industrialised nations is holding back the developing world?

Thinking big and building big is off the international development agenda, along with autonomous decision-making by African governments. In keeping with the mantra of 'sustainability', by which is meant cautious, small-scale, local, minimal development with limited environmental impact, the UN and G8 nations are promoting their Millennium Development Goals (MDGs). Launched in 2000, the goals are intended to ensure a 50 per cent reduction in the numbers living in extreme poverty – defined as less than a dollar a day – by 2015. But what happens to the other half? And in any case, this really means keeping people alive rather than the serious development needed to ensure a decent life. In so far as desperately needed infrastructure gets a look in, it is also considered from a survivalist perspective. In a telling speech, the World Bank vice-president for private sector and infrastructure even felt it appropriate to cite British shipments of prisoners to Australia as a useful historical precedent for the 'outcome-based contracts' now required for infrastructure development: 90 per cent of prisoners died before reaching Australian shores until captains were paid for each prisoner who arrived alive.[1]

Debt relief and aid are seen as a key means to achieve MDG 'targets' and 'outcomes'. African governments are treated like bad parents, in need of behaviour-modification programmes, to make them look after their poor. Many campaigners and commentators have decried the paltry increase in aid agreed at the G8 summit, but, in contrast, the MDGs are widely commended despite the low horizons they embody. Worse still, the level of interference in developing countries and the regulation involved is positively welcomed.

Debt relief, which acts as both carrot and stick, has been given a fanfare, yet for the 14 poorest African countries it merely rubber-stamps the current position, as these countries cannot afford their repayments anyway. It releases no new major funds, and recipient countries have to 'redistribute' the funds they don't have to 'poverty-reduction programmes' that fit Western priorities.

Ghana provides a good example. It is a stable sub-Saharan country and, having met the criteria for Highly Indebted Poor Country (HIPC) status, is now qualified for debt relief. It is almost the same size geographically as the UK, but with a population of only 20.7 million, and GDP per capita of £1280 ($2300), compared to the UK's £16,445 ($29,600).[2]

Under HIPC, Ghana's debt relief amounts to a saving of £132.9 million annually in debt service costs.[3] This amounts to approximately £6.65p per Ghanaian per year, or level of 'debt forgiveness' of just under 2p a day each. Given that 60 per cent of Ghanaians remain in subsistence farming, this is more about transforming the image of Western leaders and dictating Ghanaian affairs than improving Ghana's prospects.

Kpachilo School in northern Ghana, built under the HIPC debt-relief scheme, proudly sports a rainbow logo with an 'HIPC Benefit' painted beneath. Repugnant in itself as a symbol suggesting 'You are the good and deserving extremely poor, be grateful', in fact the school cannot attract qualified teachers, not only due to lack of pay, but because there are no adequate roads to the school, no running water and no electricity. Similarly, localised boreholes dug with miserly debt-relief funds dry up and quickly become unsanitary due to inadequate aquifers.

While the West feels better for its gesture, and the poorest countries bow to Western diktats, the investment that is really needed is not campaigned for. Foreign direct investment (FDI) inflows into the whole of Africa are only 3 per cent of the total global flow of FDI.[4] But campaigning for investment is unlikely to attract pop stars, non-governmental organisations (NGOs) and public sympathy. In addition, to suggest that resources should be expended on industrial development, huge road networks, electrification, and major water or sanitation plants is untrendy in the West.

The West African gas pipeline project, for example, which will pipe gas through an 800-kilometre (500-mile) pipeline from Nigeria and supply Benin, Togo and Ghana for electricity

Open-cast gold mining in the Ashanti gold fields. Security is necessary to prevent local people stealing basic building materials like polythene sheets for roofing.

generation, has met considerable opposition from NGOs. Objections range from claims that the scheme will create communal strife, and that villages or ecosystems will be destroyed, to concerns that the piped gas will be used for industrial purposes.[5] Despite the fact that 90 per cent of Ghanaian households still have to burn wood or charcoal to cook, Friends of the Earth, in a media briefing in May this year, claimed that 'the region already has a sufficient power supply', and is concerned that mining will be a key beneficiary of the pipeline.[6]

In fact, in Ghana only 45 per cent of the population has access to electricity at all, compared to 100 per cent in the UK. In rural areas it is even worse, with only 7.5 per cent having access to electricity.[7] Most rural Africans live in darkness. The annual electricity consumption per capita in Ghana is approximately 300 KWh compared to 6158 KWh per capita in the UK. This allows each Ghanaian to run an air-conditioner for four months of the year, provided they don't have any other appliances at all, or a colour television, or one fridge for less than half a year – but none of these at the same time, or in the same year.[8]

Mining, which is vital to Ghana's economy, providing over £176.7 million in revenues through tax and royalties to the government each year,[9] urgently needs a reliable power supply. This is worth more annually than debt relief, but greens and anti-poverty campaigners alike are profoundly hostile to mining, regardless of the revenues it creates or jobs it provides. Ghana is Africa's second largest gold producer. It is also a major producer of bauxite, manganese and diamonds. Constant power supplies to mining operations have been disrupted in Ghana due to drought, which has reduced the Volta River levels that feed the Volta dam, whose hydroelectric scheme has until recently supplied most of Ghana's electricity supply. This has resulted in a drop in production levels for many mining operations. In a similar vein, VALCO, an aluminium smelting plant that was employing over 1500 workers at its peak as one of Ghana's few major industries, was forced to close in 2003 due to electricity shortages and spiralling power costs. It remains in limbo while negotiations for a buy-out continue. Its problems attracted no complaints from NGOs or campaigners because industrial development does not fit the Western emphasis on the small, local and basic needs ethos of 'extreme poverty reduction' and 'sustainable development'.

Beyond the aid, trade and debt-relief concerns of development NGOs and Western government leaders, with all their poverty-reduction 'conditionalities', private investors are also making too many excuses. Commentators often argue that the obstacles to development are cultural, and that outdated forms of property ownership, corruption and tradition keep FDI flowing elsewhere. While across Africa the demand is there for everything from prefabricated homes to replace the desperate mud huts, to shopping malls and modern transport systems, many Westerners wrongly presume that much of the status quo is a matter of cultural tradition, with poverty a product of corrupt regimes. In Africa, mud huts are not romantic bolt holes, and subsistence farming is not a career choice. These are not traditions anyone wants to preserve. It is indisputable that people in the developing world want the best the West has, from big fast cars to Minimalist designer apartments with jacuzzis. Yet amidst the poverty it is assumed that anyone who has these things must be corrupt, so that investing in their development is 'cultural imperialism'. Such discourse justifies the grim view that little is possible, that Africans can't be trusted and need lessons in 'good governance'. This all further justifies debilitating Western interference.

Campaigning for political autonomy and major investment may be the most important 'awareness raising' we could do in the West, rather than the Live 8/G8 jamborees that mobilise pity and deny people in the developing world the freedom to build big, develop and contribute to the world. ⚙

Notes
1. Nemat Shafik, 'Making Infrastructure Work for the Poor', the World Bank Group, February 2002. www.worldbank.org, accessed 21 July 2005.
2. Central Intelligence Agency, *The World Factbook 2004*. www.cia.gov/cia/publications/factbook/rankorder/2004 rank.html, accessed 21 July 2005.
3. News release 2005/21/PREM. www.worldbank.org, accessed 21 July 2005.
4. United Nations Conference on Trade and Development, 'World FDI flows grew an estimated 6% in 2004, ending downturn', UNCTAD press release (UNCTAD/Press/PR/2005/002/11/1/200 5). www.unctad.org, accessed 8 August 2005.

5. http://brettonwoodsproject.org, accessed 21 July 2005.
6. Friends of the Earth, 'Development and the West African Gas Pipeline', media briefing, 18–20 May 2005. www.foe.co.uk/resource/media_briefin g/development_aid_and_the_we.pdf, accessed 8 August 2005.
7. 'International Energy Agency World Energy Outlook 2002'. www.worldenergyoutlook.org, accessed 21 July 2005.
8. www.galapagos.solarquest.com, accessed 21 July 2005.
9. 'Ghana Minerals Commission 2002'. www.mincomgh.org, accessed 21 July 2005.

Appreciating Cumbernauld

Built between 1961 and 1969, Cumbernauld town centre was intended by the town's newly established architects' department to be the centrepiece of a Modernist 'utopia' that would absorb Glasgow's overspill. It initially attracted architectural honours, but coverage then became damning. Reyner Banham said of it: 'It shaped its times, and was shaped by them, most notably and depressingly in the use of raw off-the-form concrete … a weeping, sweeping, drip-stained brown.'[1] As a visiting professor at the University of Strathclyde, **Gordon Murray** has worked with the head of the school, Steven Spier, to focus all final-year projects on Cumbernauld. This has resulted in a reappraisal and reappreciation of the much-maligned megastructure.

Whenever technology reaches its real fulfilment it transcends into architecture.
— Mies van der Rohe, 'Architecture and technology', 1955[2]

Harold Wilson's 'white heat of technology' marks the zenith of the last millennium for many observers, with Neil Armstrong's moon walk of 1969, only five years away, along with Biafra, My Lai and Charles Manson.

In Scotland, this technology was manifest in the Forth Road Bridge, Ben Cruachan Hydro-electric Station deep in the mountains of Argyll, and the vast colliery vents and winding gear designed by Egon Riss at the National Coal Board. Hovering in the background was one of Scotland's most enlightened 'future thinkers', the late Sir Robert Grieve from the Scottish Development Department, whose positive influence in transforming Scotland's urban landscapes in the 1960s cannot be overstated.

Yet these were but stops on the journey from William Arroll's railway bridge over the Forth to the Falkirk Wheel, itself fusing the engineering of an earlier age linking the Union and Forth+Clyde canals.

The theories of Cedric Price and Archigam, embodied in the polyvalent Centre Pompidou by Piano and Rogers, surely reached final resolution in the oil platforms of the North Sea. The Ninian storage and production platform constructed in Nigg Bay in 1975 was the largest movable structure on earth. In this lineage lies Cumbernauld town centre, its ancestors undoubted, its parenthood clarified in this piece. It was a unique event in the history of urban design in Scotland and recognised as such by the American Institute of Architects in

Models showing how the first phase of the town centre was to be extended.

**Geoffrey Copcutt, Cumbernauld town
centre under construction, 1966**
View of main approach to the centre
from the south.

1967. The RS Reynolds Memorial Award for Community
Architecture citation was that Cumbernauld was 'the most
significant contribution to the art and science of urban design
in the western world',[3] and only made possible by those
radical powers presented by the New Town legislation.

Guiseppe Terragni, the Italian Rationalist architect writing
in *La Casabella* in March 1930 about his housing project, the
Novocomum in Como, set out a manifesto for his building
that is a precursor for the theory of Cumbernauld town
centre: 'This building, the first organic and exhaustive
example of rationalist architecture, has proved to be an
excellent *machine à habiter* ... The abolition of walls as
structural elements creates the possibility of stripping the
division between one room and the next of that fixed and
unchanging character typical of the old constructions. The
wall may thus be moveable, composed of light,
interchangeable elements. Moreover, the opportunity to
create enormous apertures has made possible new, previously
unthinkable and suggestive relationships between the
building and the landscape around it.'[4]

In the early part of the 1960s a number of views on the
machine à habiter, as described by Terragni, were coalescing.
Cumbernauld is the one construction in Scotland where these
theories become reality.

Nicholas Habraken, who Banham recognised as the most
passionate megastructuralist in demanding that citizens
should help create their own environment was, after the
publication of *Supports: An Alternative to Mass Housing*, first
in Dutch in 1961 and then in English in 1972,[5] 'something of
a guru'.[6] Habraken's idea that 'we should not try to forecast
what will happen, but try to make provision for the
unforeseen'[7] can be compared with Price's theory of 'an
architecture of calculated uncertainty ... as it is not the
architects role to crystal gaze'.[8] Or to Copcutt's 'provision for
the future where flexibility reflects accelerating change'.[9]

This was an embryonic architecture exemplifying the

theoretical in Habraken's work, or that of Price in his 1965
Fun Palace project – 'a socially interactive machine
integrating concepts of technological interchangeability with
social participation, in which citizens could entertain and
educate themselves by assembling their own environments',[10]
and out of which its underlying reason becomes evident. This
was a framework to support the ever-changing variety that is
the human experience. Habraken proposed the separation of
the 'support' or base building from the 'infill' or interior fit-
out,[11] which became treated as separate entities with different
lifecycles in order to build an environment that can respond
to individual needs. It supports user participation,
industrialisation and a restructuring of the building process,
and as such has much in common with the theories of 'open
building', as Stephen Kendall and Jonathan Teicher recognise
in *Residential Open Building*.[12]

By 1969, Cumbernauld had been evolving for eight years –
seven in design and construction. I first visited in 1967 as a
16-year-old. It appeared to me, then, and again five years later
when I returned as an architecture student, that it was the
one place in our country where you might look through the
tear in the fabric of a 19th-century Presbyterian Scotland, still
the core of all our postwar towns, and glimpse the 21st
century.

Others across the world also saw this light, and made great
journeys to understand the experiment that was going on
here. As if attuned to the echoes of 20 centuries from this
outpost of Antonine's Roman legions, Pier Luigi Nervi turned
up to see Cumbernauld, as did Banham. Another visitor, Lewis
Mumford, comments in his essay for the *Architectural Record*
of 1963 ('Social complexity and urban design'), that 'if there
has been a flaw in this development it is only that it has
proceeded so rapidly that it has not been able to incorporate
the result of past experiments and recent urban experience.'[13]

However, the analysis was deep, and assimilated a mass of
accumulated data. Copcutt recalls: 'I shamelessly did night-

Cumbernauld town centre nearing completion in 1967. Eschewing the mainly 19th-century village of Cumbernauld and its medieval origins located in a valley to the north, the new town set its centre on the hill top following a more Mediterranean medieval model: the Italian hill town.

The wonderfully elegant concrete forms of the centre here in construction in 1963 were unique in Scotland, with power-supply engineering such as the huge winding gear and vents designed for coalmines by Egon Riss.

classes in poaching statistics and traffic planning. By day we engaged academics in a 100-town social/retail study and spent weekends sampling wind and earth. In between we debated income and spending patterns, projected travel modes, and deliveries whilst juggling structural grids to match parking modules, mitigating Venturi effects and all the while, like a jeweller fashioning precious metal, I hammered the cross sections and shaped landscape to forge an urban morphology.'[14]

Reyner Banham, writing in *The Age of the Masters,* notes: 'What has been built so far is a small fraction of Copcutt's original design, but it seems all that is going to be built in this particular mega-mode.'[15]

Cumbernauld was designed not just as a shopping centre, but as a town, although the supermarket was the largest in Scotland on completion. It was like an Italian hill town – the San Gimingano of the Campsies – and this Copcutt saw as a paradox: 'the open citadel'. Twenty years later, and no less sure of the importance of the vision, replying to Banham, Copcutt wrote: 'This fragment ... is still big enough to define a future.'[16] In Δ in May 1963, Copcutt defines that future in a mission statement, which reads like something from a Fritz Lang film script: 'On the ridge and upper southern slope of the hill will rise a single citadel-like structure, half a mile long, 200 yards wide and up to eight storeys high ... Elevated over a unidirectional vehicular system, this multilevel development, with provision for most of the commercial civic religious cultural and recreational uses for a population of 70,000, will be the largest single employment source.

'The flexibility reflects accelerating change in retail and entertainment patterns. The centre could become a gigantic vending machine through which the motorized user drives to return revictualled or remotely it could be turned to industrial production.

'At the east end of the centre is the large span entertainment building connected down to the bus terminus and capable of subdivision. This structure, which is a further extension of the decks, will include auditoria, bowling lanes, dance floors, cafes and gardens. At the heart of the centre is a multi-purpose gallery for lectures concerts and meetings which can also accommodate exhibitions.'[17]

A cursory analysis of the original drawings (held in a factory archive on the edge of the town) reveals the beautiful clarity of the original intentions: nurseries, library, social club, welfare and support organisations, town squares, hotels as well as, Copcutt also reveals, 'a mosaic of sites I had tucked in for flea-markets'.

He goes on: 'This fragment was shorn of its second row of pylons and pent-housing, cradled on a protective umbrella structure, with a host of functional and spatial consequences – the winter-garden front to the tiers of offices, the tube roof illuminating the chapel, the glistening airplane wing which was to have tilted over the library and even the wall of dwellings with upper promenade designed to curtain the parkland.'[18]

Unfortunately 'supports' implies a long-term rationale underlying a layer of continuing change, evolution or churn that is a modern adaptable city. Cumbernauld was never allowed to develop that rationale. Instead, it was measured against the crude mechanics of 1970s retail theory and found wanting. The clarity of the idea is now lost in a series of corrosive interventions leading up to the end of the century, which enveloped it in layer after layer of meaningless retail concepts to the extent that understanding its very nature is now an archaeological exercise.

It is ironic that by utilising an ignored part of the original vision, that calculated uncertainty principle, the science of consumption, nowadays much more sophisticated, would have been more capable of responding to the subtleties of the centre.

At the closing of the millennium, where timescales are measured in milliseconds against a four-minute attention span, the idea that something permanent – supports – might only provide an armature around which short-term desires could be realised was an alien concept. The only idea of flexibility implied a black box – no discipline, no rationale.

The town centre approaching its opening (circa 1967) in 1968. Originally planned with two linear high-level residential 'streets', and with the capacity for two further phases to be replicated to the east and west, only the first phase was ever constructed.

Cover from the issue on Cumbernauld town centre, *Architectural Design*, May 1963.

Copcutt's original montage from *AD* of the town-centre model and the epitome of the era of the car and mass consumption: the American drophead saloon. Ironically, rather than dominating or defining, Copcutt saw the car tamed in his vision.

The unique idea, separated from the technology available for its realisation as in much of Scotland's postwar 'innovation', can be revitalised by technologies available today. For example, the same spread of fire regulations that led to much of the double-height spaces and galleries being enclosed would today, with the application of modern technology, permit an unpacking to be carried out.

It is ironic (that word crops up a lot when considering this town) that the lack of critical mass of indigenous population sadly lacking in, and responsible for, much of the malaise of the original centre has been dramatically reversed in the 'exurban' growth on the edge of the town. However, as with the linear city that is Clyde-Forth, currently coalescing along the fringes of the M8, critical mass is no longer a guarantee of positive change in the future for any of Scotland's towns, or of a reversal in their decline. Habraken summarises this eloquently in his section in *Supports* entitled 'The modern nomad':

'We have to make possible the creation of districts which may grow old without becoming obsolete, which can absorb the latest ideas and yet have a sense of history. Districts in which the population can live for generations and which yet incorporate the potential for change'.[19] *AD*

Notes
1. Reyner Banham, *Megastructure: Urban Futures of the Recent Past,* Thames and Hudson (London), 1976, pp 168–9.
2. Mies van der Rohe, 'Architecture and technology', *Perspecta*, Yale University, 1955.
3. RS Reynolds Memorial Award for Community Architecture, established 1966, and announced by the American Institute of Architects, *aia Journal*, July 1967, cited in Frederic J Osborn and Arnold Whittick, *The New Towns: The Answer to Megalopolis*, Leonard Hill (London), 1969, with an introduction by Lewis Mumford, p 386, first published 1963.
4. Attilio Terragni, Daniel Libeskind and Paolo Rosselli, *The Terragni Atlas: Built Architecture*, Skira (Milan), 2005.
5. Nicholas Habraken, *Supports: An Alternative to Mass Housing*, Architectural Press (London), 1972.
6. Reyner Banham, *Megastructure: Urban Futures of the Recent Past,* Thames and Hudson (London), 1976), p 9.
7. Habraken, op cit.
8. See Samantha Hardingham, *Cedric Price – Opera*, Wiley-Academy (Chichester), 2003.
9. Geoffrey Copcutt, 'Cumbernauld Town Centre in Retrospect', 1995, reprinted in Miles Glendinning (ed), *Rebuilding Scotland: The Post-War Vision 1945–1975*, Tuckwell Press (Edinburgh), 1997.
10. *Cedric Price – Opera*, op cit.
11. www.habraken.com, accessed 25 July 2005.
12. Stephen Kendall and Jonathan Teicher, *Residential Open Building*, E&FN Spon (London), 2000.
13 Lewis Mumford, 'Social complexity and urban design', *Architectural Record*, 1963.
14. Copcutt, op cit.
15. Reyner Banham, *The Age of the Masters: A Personal View of Modern Architecture*, Harper Trade (New York), 1975.
16. Copcutt, op cit.
17. L Hugh Wilson, DR Leaker and Geoffrey Copcutt, 'Cumbernauld New Town Central Area'. Description by Geoffrey Copcutt. Reprinted from *AD* 1963.
18. Ibid.
19. Habraken, op cit.

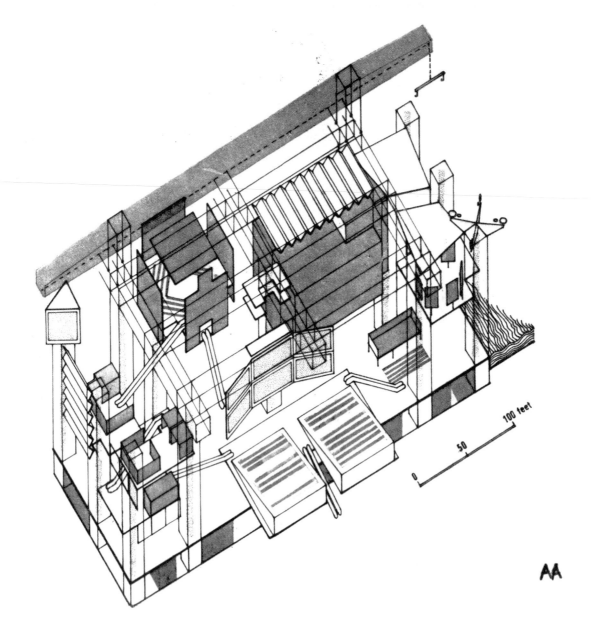

Cedric Price: From the 'Brain Drain' to the 'Knowledge Economy'

Stanley Mathews looks at Cedric Price's Fun Palace and Potteries Thinkbelt as polemics addressing the changing economic and social character of postwar Britain moving into a period of deindustrialisation, with the expansion of higher education, and the emergence of information technology.

Cedric Price, Fun Palace, 1964
Cedric Price and structural engineer Frank Newby designed a structural matrix with
overhead cranes to allow assembly of prefabricated modules.

In his 1626 book *New Atlantis*, Sir Francis Bacon described a mythical utopia, an ideal society of learning and scientific advancement. The centrepiece of this New Atlantis was 'Salomon's House', which amounted to a technical college dedicated to scientific research into 'the knowledge of causes, and secret motions of things; and the enlarging of the bounds of human empire, to the effecting of all things possible.'[1]

There are striking similarities between Bacon's New Atlantis and the late British architect Cedric Price's Fun Palace and Potteries Thinkbelt. In their respective projects, both Bacon and Price proposed new modes of knowledge and inquiry that rejected established systems of education and thought. Both men confronted a crisis of knowledge at a time of paradigm shift. In Bacon's time, this was England's transition from a medieval worldview that revered received knowledge and ancient authority, to an era of modern methods of scientific inquiry. For Price, it was an awareness of an epistemological shift from the structures and traditions of Britain of the First Machine Age to the postindustrial, postimperial era of information technology and the knowledge economy.

In his 1964 Fun Palace and the 1967 Potteries Thinkbelt projects, Price addressed what he perceived to be the new and rapidly changing conditions of knowledge and society in postwar Britain. These were not proposals for buildings in any conventional sense, but were instead impermanent,

improvisational and interactive systems, highly adaptable to the volatile social and economic conditions of their time and place. At a time of uncertainty and instability, Price's work reflects a new approach to architecture as a site of change and impermanence, rather than as permanent and monumental symbols of cultural cohesion and consensus.

When Price first met avant-garde theatre producer Joan Littlewood in 1962, she described her ideas for a new kind of theatre. From her beginnings in working-class agit-prop street theatre to her string of successes on the London stage with her Theatre Workshop, Littlewood had longed to create a theatre of pure performativity, a space of cultural bricolage where people could experience the transcendence and transformation of the theatre not as audience, but as players themselves. Her innovative vision provided the conceptual framework on which Price began to design an interactive, performative architecture, endlessly adaptable to the varying needs and desires of the users. Working in collaboration, Price and Littlewood developed the Fun Palace as a 'university of the streets',[2] providing educational opportunities in the guise of leisure entertainment in order to prepare society for the advent of the technological age. It was an improvisational architecture endlessly in the process of construction, dismantling and reassembly.

Price and avant-garde theatre producer Joan Littlewood conceived of the Fun Palace as a 'university of the streets', combining entertainment and education.

Cedric Price, InterAction Centre, Kentish Town, 1976
Price's InterAction Centre incorporated many of the concepts and features of the ill-fated Fun Palace but on a much-reduced scale. It provided community services and creative outlets for local citizens until its demolition in 2003. In 1977, Reyner Banham noted Price's influence on the design of the Centre Pompidou, writing: 'The concept of a stack of clear floors that can be adapted to a variety of cultural and recreational functions seems to recall the … Fun Palace of Cedric Price and Joan Littlewood, even if the project was never as radical as the floorless Fun Palace, or as casually innovatory as Price's InterAction Centre.' [14]

The working-class population of east London could use cranes and prefabricated modules to assemble learning and leisure environments, creating spaces where they might escape everyday routine and embark on a journey of creativity and personal development. The ideas for the Fun Palace were, in many respects, similar to the 'spontaneous university' that Price and Littlewood's mutual friend, the Scottish 'Beat' poet and situationist Alexander Trocchi, was also proposing at the same time. Trocchi described his project as 'a vital laboratory for the creation (and evaluation) of conscious situations … it is not only the environment which is in question, plastic, subject to change, but people also.' [3] It is clear that while Price and Littlewood influenced Trocchi's project, Trocchi's situationist ideas on creativity and improvisation also helped to shape the developing Fun Palace.

Price and Littlewood enlisted a cadre of scientists, sociologists, artists, engineers and politicians, including Richard Buckminster Fuller, Yehudi Menuhin, Gordon Pask and Tony Benn, to help with the Fun Palace. Their ambitious goal was to create an interactive environment, a new kind of architecture, capable of altering its form to accommodate the changing needs of the users. Using cybernetics and the latest computer technologies, Price hoped to create an improvisational architecture that would be capable of learning, anticipating and adapting to the constantly evolving programme. An array of sensors and inputs would provide real-time feedback on use and occupancy to computers that would allocate and alter spaces and resources according to projected needs.

A site was chosen for the Fun Palace, on the banks of the Lea River in London's East End. However, after years of development and design, construction was blocked by mid-level bureaucrats in the Newham planning office. Price and Littlewood struggled to overcome bureaucratic opposition to the Fun Palace until 1975, when Price declared the then 10-year-old project obsolete. However, the failure of the Fun Palace was not the end of Price's attempts to realise an interactive and improvisational architecture. In 1976, he built a greatly reduced version of the Fun Palace in Kentish Town. Known as the InterAction Centre, this design incorporated many of the features and innovations of the Fun Palace, though on a smaller scale. It resembled a 'bargain basement' version of Centre Pompidou and, along with the Fun Palace, influenced Richard Roger's designs.

Even before the final demise of the Fun Palace, Price had begun work on an even more vast and far-sighted project. His 1966 Potteries Thinkbelt was a plan to convert a region of the UK's once-thriving industrial heartland into a 260-square-kilometre (100-square-mile) think tank, recuperating derelict industrial sites and railways as the basic infrastructure for a

Price proposed using the derelict rail network of the Potteries as the basic infrastructure for a new 'educational industry' to replace the old manufacturing economy

Cedric Price, Potteries Thinkbelt, regional site plan, 1966
The North Staffordshire Potteries were once a centre for the British ceramics industry and home to such famous names as Wedgwood, Spode and Minton. But by the 1960s they had fallen into ruin and rust, the victims of rising costs and foreign competition. Price proposed using the derelict rail network of the Potteries as the basic infrastructure for a new 'educational industry' to replace the old manufacturing economy. More than a dozen small towns were incorporated into the Thinkbelt, which covered more than 260 square kilometres (100 square miles). Price hoped that the Potteries Thinkbelt would help to reverse the tide of the Brain Drain and put the nation at the forefront of advanced technologies. (Colour keys added by the author for clarity.)

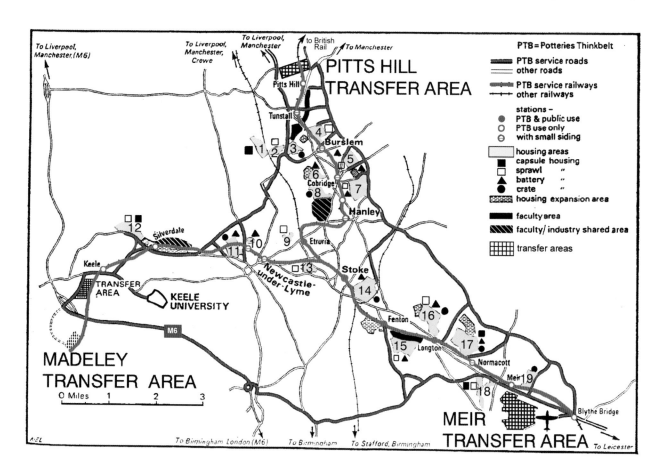

new 'educational industry', in part to stem the tide of the Brain Drain.

Like many industries in England, the coal and ceramics industries of North Staffordshire had fallen on hard times after the Second World War and, by the 1960s, the Potteries was a ruined industrial landscape. The conditions were repeated in scores of industrial centres throughout the UK, and as early as 1960 the situation had become so alarming that Labour MP Anthony Crosland publicly complained to the House of Commons: 'Our production and export performance is almost the poorest of any advanced industrial country ... much of our technical education [is] equally backward. We cling to every outmoded scrap of national sovereignty, continue to play the obsolete role of an imperial power, and fail to adjust to the new dynamic Europe.'[4]

Price sought to re-establish the North Staffordshire Potteries as a centre of science and emerging technologies, much as they had been during the Industrial Revolution. He envisioned his Potteries Thinkbelt as a wholesale conversion of England's rusting industrial infrastructure into a new 'industry' of technical education and scientific research, focusing on practical applications.

A 1964 article from the *Times* Educational Supplement, entitled 'Noddyland Atmosphere?', quoted Price as saying that British universities were out of touch with current social, economic and scientific conditions.[5] He avoided referring to his Thinkbelt project as a 'university' because he disliked the upper-class connotations of the word, and complained that English universities were little more than 'medieval castles with power points, located in gentlemanly seclusion'.[6] In 1966, Price wrote that 'further education and re-education must be viewed as a major industrial undertaking and not as a service run by gentlemen for the few'.[7]

Despite the promises of postwar educational reform by both the Labour and Conservative governments, British higher education in the postwar years was still largely associated with prestige, high social status and the classics, lagging far behind western Europe and the US in research opportunities and technical training.[8]

Even in the new 'redbrick' universities that sprang up across the UK in the postwar years, pure science and theoretical research were privileged over technical education and applied science. A mandate for new universities to boost economic development failed to produce any significant economic improvement, for while educational authorities acknowledged a correlation between education and national economic development, they remained oddly sceptical about the relevance of technical and scientific education to industrial progress.[9] In a 1965 House of Lords debate on the lack of technical education, Lord Aberdare complained: 'I have a feeling that the universities ... are still inclined to give greater importance to the arts than to the sciences, and to the academic than to the technological. There still exists a kind of intellectual snobbery that pays greater respect to the man who misquotes Horace than the man who can repair his own car.'[10]

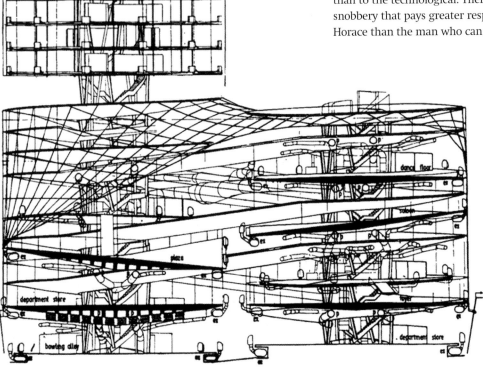

Mike Webb, Sin Centre, London, proposed section, 1959 to 1961
The only contemporary project that came close to the spirit of Price's work was Webb's Sin Centre, an innovative entertainment centre for the site of the Empire Theatre in Leicester Square, London. Pedestrian and vehicle circulation were brought together along spiralling ramps, and most of the structure was wrapped in a tensile skin of plastic and steel cables. Although the Sin Centre predates the Fun Palace, Webb doubts that his ideas had any significant impact on Price's designs for that project.

Price coined the neologism 'thinkbelt' to describe the educational orientation as well as the regional scale of his project, describing it as 'a kind of cross between Berkeley in California and a College of Advanced Technology', for 20,000 students.[11] He hoped that his Potteries Thinkbelt would help to break down the traditional wall between 'pure' and 'applied' science and technology, lure scientists and technologists back to the UK, and help to put the nation at the forefront of advanced technologies.[12]

His plan for the Potteries Thinkbelt was to utilise the abandoned rail network of the Potteries as the infrastructure of his new think tank. Using the technologies of prefabrication and containerised shipping, he designed mobile, rail-mounted classrooms, computer and data storage modules, laboratories, and lecture and demonstration halls, which would shunt constantly from place to place along the refurbished railway lines.

At three locations, Price designed large transfer stations where the mobile modules could be assembled and moved using enormous gantry cranes. He also designed 19 immense housing complexes using four types of prefabricated, modular housing units: 'capsule', 'sprawl', 'crate' and 'battery'.

In all, there were to be 32,000 living units.[13] Like the mobile teaching units, the housing modules could be moved around and rearranged by cranes and rail as the programme changed over time. Students could leave their homes in the morning, board the mobile classrooms, and learn while their classroom moved along the Potteries Thinkbelt rail circuit, from a demonstration laboratory, to a model factory, to an experimental station, returning back to their modular homes at the end of the day. Price's plan defined an interactive network of static and mobile structures, inspired and controlled by emergent computer and information technologies on which new social, economic and industrial patterns might develop. The mobile learning units were like information quanta, the switches and transfer stations like the logical gateways of a vast computer circuit. The Potteries Thinkbelt defined a new kind of architectural monumentality, not of large object-buildings, but as a vast and dispersed field of discrete objects and disparate events.

In the Potteries Thinkbelt, Price enlarged on the improvisational, adaptable model of architecture he had first explored in the Fun Palace to create a landscape of constant change and activity, more like an electronic circuit than a static building. His redeployment of the ruined industrial landscape of the Potteries was a microcosm of his vision for architecture and for the future of the UK (a radical departure from the stolid monuments of traditional universities or the new redbrick schools), offering new models of economic, educational and social development within an active architectural matrix far more extensive than that of the Fun Palace.

Like the Fun Palace, the Potteries Thinkbelt was never realised. Price had never identified a client for it, and his proposal failed to attract much more than bemused interest.

The technical complexity of the project seemed too far-fetched to a public and a government unfamiliar with computers and advanced technology. Moreover, many of the government officials who might have been interested in Price's novel educational ideas were otherwise occupied with the development of the fledgling Open University.

Price recognised that the UK was in an irreversible cycle of deindustrialisation and, in order to remain competitive in an increasingly technological world, nothing less than a complete reorientation of the British system of higher education towards science and information technology would be required. Yet he also realised that the mercurial conditions of the postwar years required a new impermanent and agile architecture, capable not only of adapting to inevitable change, but of encouraging and advancing social transformation. Price's radical redefinition of architecture has influenced architects since the early 1960s, when he took on the role of avuncular guru to the young members of Archigram. In the Fun Palace and Potteries Thinkbelt, Price emerged as one of the first architects to develop innovative architectural responses to the new social and economic conditions of postwar Britain. ⌂

Notes
1. Sir Francis Bacon, *The New Atlantis*, 1626.
2. Joan Littlewood, 'A laboratory of fun', *New Scientist*, 14 May 1964, pp 432–3.
3. Alexander Trocchi, 'A revolutionary proposal: Invisible insurrection of a million minds', first published as 'Technique du coupe du monde', *Internationale Situationniste 8*, January 1963.
4. Anthony Crosland, 'Encounter', October 1960, quoted in Christopher Booker, *The Neophiliacs: A Study of the Revolution in English Life in the Fifties and Sixties*, Collins (London), 1969, p 153.
5. Peter Laslett and Cedric Price, 'Noddyland Atmosphere?', *Times Educational Supplement*, 29 May 1964, Potteries Thinkbelt document folio DR1995:0216:400, Cedric Price Archives, Canadian Centre for Architecture, Montreal.
6. Cedric Price, 'Life conditioning', *Architectural Design 36*, October 1966, p 483.
7. Cedric Price, 'Potteries Thinkbelt: A plan for an advanced educational industry in North Staffordshire', *Architectural Design* op cit, pp 484–97.
8. Michael Sanderson, *Education and Economic Decline in Britain, 1870s to the 1990s*, Cambridge University Press (Cambridge), 1999, p 81.
9. Martin Weiner, *English Culture and the Decline of the Industrial Spirit, 1850–1980*, Cambridge University Press (New York), 1982.
10. Lord Aberdare, 'Response to Lord Robbins' Statements on Higher Education', *Parliamentary Debates, House of Lords Official Report 270:12*, HMSO (London), Wednesday, 1 December 1965), col 1281, Fun Palace document folio MS1995:0188, Cedric Price Archives, Canadian Centre for Architecture, Montreal.
11. Cedric Price, 'Potteries Thinkbelt' (unpublished manuscript), February 1966, p 2, Potteries Thinkbelt document folio DR1995:0216:400, Cedric Price Archives, Canadian Centre for Architecture, Montreal.
12. Cedric Price, 'Potteries Thinkbelt: A plan for an advanced educational industry in North Staffordshire', *Architectural Design* op cit, p 484.
13. Cedric Price, '10.3 Housing Areas: Unit Provision', in 'Potteries Thinkbelt' (unpublished manuscript), op cit.
14. Reyner Banham, 'Centre Pompidou', *Architectural Review 161*, May 1977, pp 270–94.

Waltropolis: City in a Box

Reyner Banham now seems premature in declaring the megastructure dead in the early 1970s. Here, **theboxtank** (**Emily Andersen**, **Geoff DeOld** and **Corey Hoelker**), a collaborative blog about big-box urbanism and retail, considers the latent architectural possibilities of the now global phenomenon of space enclosing industrially clad megasheds – the potential of which was never underestimated by Cedric Price or Martin Pawley.

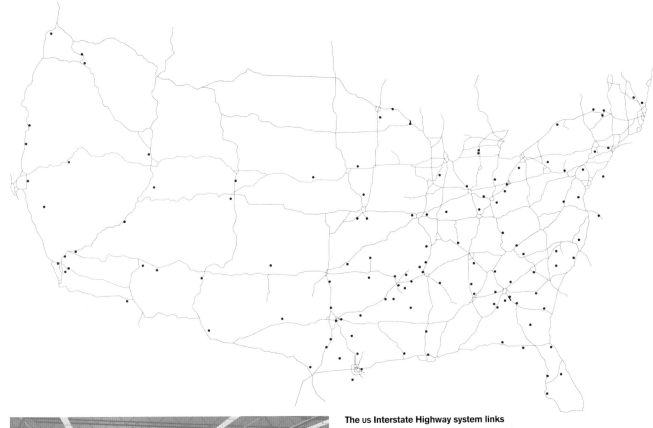

The US Interstate Highway system links Wal-Mart's 117 distribution centres, which are located in close proximity to this massive piece of infrastructure. The controlled-access freeway system allows Wal-Mart's private fleet of semi-tractor trailers to move merchandise uninterrupted so that it is in continual motion from point of order to point of sale.

The infinite interior of discount space, a precondition for 'Always Low Prices', continues throughout all Supercenters and Wal-Mart stores.

The largest retailer in the world, Wal-Mart, has become host to an increasing variety of public functions as its Supercenters grow in size. Wal-Mart's brand of development and stand-alone, single-destination big-box stores have become suburban megastructures. Located at the periphery of cities, these big boxes are shifting the shopping experience away from the model that replaced Main Street: the shopping mall. Wal-Mart's competition-killing organisational and distribution systems have created what one might call 'discount space', a place where the experiential mode of shopping is replaced with 'Always Low Prices – Always'.[1]

Wal-Mart is Big, Wal-Mart is Distribution

Wal-Mart is the biggest company in the world. Wal-Mart's net income and sales revenue in the fiscal year ending 31 January 2005 were $10.3 billion and $285.2 billion respectively.[2] Wal-Mart's GDP situates it between Austria and Saudi Arabia as the 23rd largest economy in the world, and it is the largest private employer in North America. Wal-Mart's 423-terabyte Teradata system, which tracks information ranging from product distribution to customer behaviour, is second in size only to that of the US

government. In the US, as of April 2005, Wal-Mart operated 1758 Supercenters, 1322 Discount Stores, 86 Neighborhood Markets and 552 Sam's Clubs, all fed by 117 distribution centres. In 2005, Wal-Mart added on average a store a day. The total land area of all its stores, distribution centres and associated parking covers over 116 square kilometres (45 square miles), as the map on pages 24 and 25 shows for comparison with London.

Wal-Mart is a distribution machine that sees life and the economy as something that can be mapped. The quantity and size of its stores are made possible by its immense information technology system; a centralised 'brain' that simultaneously maps, tracks, predicts, alerts, adapts, directs and coordinates the Wal-Mart machine based on conditions that are always in flux around the shifting behaviour of its customers. The importance of information trumps inventory. It is a pull-driven methodology: supply is determined by the tracking of merchandise and sales rather than from quantity of stock held in warehouses or back rooms. The Interstate Highway System links regional distribution centres with stores, a fluid network that supports Wal-Mart's privately held fleet of trucks. Inventory is in continual motion from point of order to point of sale.

Everyday scenes from a typical Wal-Mart
Clockwise, from top left: Comparing low prices in the apparel department; the parking lot at this Sam's Club is used for grilling hot dogs; Wal-Mart TV is the fifth largest television network in the US; the Wal-Mart Supercenter and the sea of parking; Piñatas, an example of the wide range of merchandise carried by the world's largest retailer; the Supercenter hosts, and provides space for, other retailers, such as McDonald's; overnight RV parking is one of the multiple nonshopping activities found in the Supercenter parking lot; Sam's Club as the extreme example of discount space.

Wal-Mart as Megastructure

Theboxtank (www.theboxtank.com) considers the latent possibilities of the big box as a megastructure, which re-emerges in the vast global network of Wal-Mart. The modular units of the Supercenter are capable of extending endlessly, both increasing the size of the individual unit and the size of the Wal-Mart network through repetition of several units on scattered sites, housing many activities associated with the changing city.[3]

The bigness of retailers like Wal-Mart depends on the increasing size of the big-box store. The big box is the ideal terminus for Wal-Mart's distribution machine. It lends itself to unlimited modularity and an expandable interiorised space. Rooted in the early warehouses and large department stores of early Modernism, its shell is expressive of the superficial mass culture of consumerism. The interior neither has any significant functional relation to an exterior, nor does it articulate differences between use and the components held within. It is a raw shell and interior fit-out with materials providing a minimum degree of finish: its sole purpose being an unarticulated mass-produced container for a mass-produced programme of mass-produced merchandise.

This shell and its accompanying retail system reproduce an efficient, flexible, functional environment that can be termed 'discount space'. Wal-Mart's slogan and ideology of 'Always Low Prices' creates an atmosphere for this space that its design reinforces. Discount space is mass-produced merchandise, arranged on standardised shelving, in a large warehouse environment where all attention is shifted towards savings. This infinitely reproduced interior is modulated by the shell of the big box, the discrete unit of discount space, which renders the box lifeless. Both inside and outside, quality is replaced with quantity and experience is replaced with economy.

All aspirations of excellence are infused with the sole purpose of discount space: savings. Every penny saved in the reproduction of the interior – in the reproduction of the system – is passed on to the consumer with lower prices.

The Supercenter, Wal-Mart's largest and most sophisticated model, offers the one-stop shopping experience. In addition to providing discount merchandise, the Supercenter includes nail and hair salons, pharmacies, banks, travel agencies, gas stations, police substations and a range of fast-food restaurants. One-stop shopping becomes one-stop urbanism as services found 'downtown' fold into the Supercenter. The residue and chance urban events of downtown have followed. Recreation vehicle (RV) parking, weddings, armed forces recruiting, voter registration, high-school marching bands, public assembly and crime (both petty and violent) converge on the Supercenter for lack of any other public infrastructure to accommodate these activities. It is privatised public space: discount style, a victory of American pragmatism. The hosting municipality no longer provides a main street or town square representing community identity. Likewise, the developer no longer provides the city with a mall serving as an anchor for public activity and gathering. A carefully distributed network of Supercenters has replaced both.

Wal-Mart's faith in its big boxes designed 60 to 100 at a time, its information technology and distribution machine allow it to create a powerful network across suburban and exurban landscapes, rendering everything in between useless to it. All that is left is to fill in the gaps. Wal-Mart is a megastructure, at the scale of an individual unit and, more important, within the milieu of retail urbanism. It is fractal in nature. Megastructure at the individual unit, and mega-infrastructure at the scale of its totality. The Supercenter is ready for a great leap forward 30 years after Reyner Banham declared 'The Megastructure is dead' in 1973, and proceeded to write its passing history.[4]

Waltropolis is 1.6 kilometres (1 mile) wide, running 11 kilometres (7 miles) along the length of any interstate highway. The roof deck accommodates suburban tract housing for a population of 100,000. Waltropolis embraces an urbanism driven by the automobile: its fundamental organisation results from a series of feeder roads, off-ramps, multitiered loading docks, and strip parking lots, all as one exit off the highway.

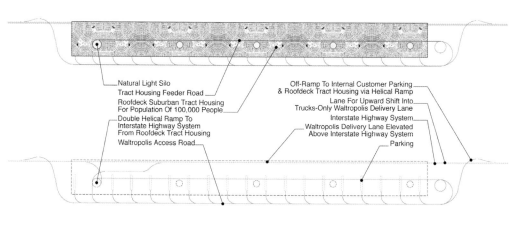

Natural Light Silo
Tract Housing Feeder Road
Roofdeck Suburban Tract Housing For Population Of 100,000 People
Double Helical Ramp To Interstate Highway System From Roofdeck Tract Housing
Waltropolis Access Road

Off-Ramp To Internal Customer Parking & Roofdeck Tract Housing via Helical Ramp
Lane For Upward Shift Into Trucks-Only Waltropolis Delivery Lane
Interstate Highway System
Waltropolis Delivery Lane Elevated Above Interstate Highway System
Parking

Waltropolis: City in a Box

In Waltropolis, a project by theboxtank, we pursue Wal-Mart's mega-infrastructural machine to a logical extension, which can only be defined as a negative utopia. Waltropolis merges all of the mechanisms of the Wal-Mart machine with the remains of the city, into the industrial complex provided by a megastructure. The city and everything contained within the city is organised in an infrastructure based on Wal-Mart's distribution machine, as a means towards the end of discount space and savings.

Waltropolis optimises the distribution of goods to its population of 100,000 people. Eleven kilometres (7 miles) long by 1.6 kilometres (1 mile) wide and 90 metres (300 feet) high, the 10 levels of Waltropolis locate the retail, civic, educational and cultural programme within the efficiency of a box, now free of conventional development patterns that limit the big box to a stand-alone entity. Repetition of the same unit occurs on separate sites. Residential tract housing is located on the roof deck, the 18 square kilometres (7 square miles) optimised to provide the suburban-style living Americans have come to expect.

Looking to maximise the efficiency of its distribution machine, Waltropolis collapses and then stacks the typical American city into multitier development. The distribution centre is eliminated, as Waltropolis is the distribution system. An extension of, and situated on, the US Interstate Highway system, Waltropolis provides its private fleet of semi-trailer trucks dedicated lanes that ramp up to loading docks. Containers are unloaded directly on to conveyer belts that transfer goods to the appropriate Waltropolis level and product department.

Movement through Waltropolis is via arterial roads that access the different levels and ramp to and from the Interstate. Thirty-six parking lots are distributed throughout two floor plates spaced every 600 metres (2000 feet). Each lot accommodates 390 regular parking spaces with 60 spaces dedicated for recreation vehicles. Each family at Waltropolis can maintain their 2.5-car lifestyle.

The greatest achievement of Waltropolis is the merging of institutions. Retail, civic, educational and cultural institutions fold into one, completing the privatisation of public institutions and their spaces. Office space, museums, classrooms, places of worship, courthouses, jails and libraries are loaded along a linear band that runs the 11-kilometre (7-mile) length of Waltropolis. All of this fronts Wal-Street, a place for parades, street fairs and other acts of public assembly that may have taken place on the traditional Main Street.

The essence of Waltropolis is the infinite expanse of horizontal space filled with shelves of merchandise. This is discount space in the extreme: urban form as a product of consumerism.

Wasted exterior space – sidewalk, park, boulevard, city square – have all been consumed by discount space and transformed to serve Waltropolis. Scattered throughout Waltropolis are restaurants, theatres, recreation fields and other entertainment spaces, providing brief distractions from shopping. This is the critical space of Waltropolis. It is here that its inhabitants are blind to the history of the city's development; to the Wal-Mart Supercenter of today, where residents of exurbia haphazardly gather for lack of adequate civic public space; and, finally, to Waltropolis, which provides everything required for contemporary urban living. ⌂

Notes
1. www.walmart.com, accessed 30 July 2005.
2. www.walmartstores.com/wm store/wmstores/HomePage.jsp, accessed 30 July 2005.
3. Reyner Banham, *Megastructure: Urban Futures of the Recent Past*, Thames and Hudson (London), 1976.
4. Reyner Banham, quoted in 'Banham: La Megastrutture e Morta', *Casabella*, No 375, March 1973, p 2.

Dedicated lanes allow semi-tractor trailers to ramp above the interstate highway directly to loading docks that serve Waltropolis's field of aisles and shelves via conveyor belts. Circular light-wells allow natural light to penetrate the depths of Waltropolis and highlight event areas.

Interchange Now

Not for them was the Modernism of neat, smooth, regular solids, notes Banham. 'The younger megastructuralists clearly saw technology as a visually wild rich mess of piping and wiring and struts and catwalks and bristling radar antennae and supplementary fuel tanks and landing-pads all carried in exposed lattice frames, NASA-style. Much of this intellectual underpinning for this picturesque view of advanced technology came, directly or otherwise, from the writings and projects of the Futurist architect Antonio Sant'Elia, in spite of the fact that he had been dead since 1916.'[1]

Appreciating Futurism, **Robert Stewart** of YRM looks at prospects for the modularisation of megastructural transport projects, having been engaged in the vast and largely subterranean development of Terminal 5 at Heathrow Airport, London. He argues for a flexible architecture in the service of mobility.

The aesthetic of the 20th-century airport has been driven by an architectural philosophy that was first developed by the Italian Futurists almost a century ago, after the Wright brothers' historic flight in 1903, but long before the first commercial aircraft flight in 1919. In 1909, and importantly before the First World War, the poet Filippo Tommaso Marinetti wrote 'The Founding and Manifesto of Futurism' for *Le Figaro* magazine,[2] praising 'the sleek flight of planes whose propellers chatter in the wind like banners and seem to cheer like an enthusiastic crowd'.[3]

These ideas were expanded by the architect Antonio Sant'Elia, who had first written a Messaggio on the problems of Modern architecture for an exhibition on the 'Città Nuova' by the group Nuove Tendenze in May 1914,[4] which he helped Marinetti turn into in the 'Manifesto of Futurist Architecture',

published in *Lacerba* in Florence in August that year. This manifesto stated that the new, or Futurist, architecture 'is the architecture of calculation, of audacious temerity and of simplicity; the architecture of reinforced concrete, of steel, glass, cardboard, textile fibre, and all those substitutes for wood, stone and brick that enable us to obtain maximum elasticity and lightness.' And that 'oblique and elliptic lines are dynamic, and by their very nature possess an emotive power a thousand times stronger than perpendiculars and horizontals, and that no integral, dynamic architecture can exist that does not include these.'[5]

A line of development derived from these ideas can be traced from Sant'Elia's sketches for an interchange in Milan that incorporated a runway above the station, through the design work of Hans Wittwer, a member of the Bauhaus

YRM, Gatwick Airport, North Terminal, 1998.

Richard Rogers, Heathrow Airport, Terminal 5 Campus, due to open 2008. Computer image by YRM.

School, at Halle-Leipzig Airport, with its cantilever form and excitement with new materials and new ways of building. In the postwar era, Minoru Yamasaki continued to explore the architecture of flight at St Louis Airport, with 'hovering' roof vaults. Then Eero Saarinen followed with the TWA Terminal at JFK Airport, New York, and most influentially at Dulles Airport, Washington. The expression of the tensions of flight continues in the work of Renzo Piano at Kansai Airport, Norman Foster at Stansted and Hong Kong Chek Lap Kok, and Richard Rogers at Madrid and Heathrow's Terminal 5.

If the Futurist movement underpins the aesthetic that dominated the 20th-century terminal, there are other ideas that are essential to the 21st-century airport.

First is the idea that 'terminal' is not an appropriate description of the building type. Its use derives from railways and shipping in that the building is seen as the culmination of the journey. An airport terminal is, however, better described as an 'interchange' between several methods of transport, a transient experience to be passed through as quickly and as effortlessly as possible.

As early as 1909, the key elements of an interchange can be seen at the flying exhibition at Frankfurt. The runway (*Propellerbahn*), a railway station and tramlines providing access for visitors, and a rapid transit system linking together the key elements of the show, are a precursor to Sant'Elia's image of the runway above the railway station in 'Statzione Aeroplani' in 1912. Early examples of built interchanges include the first terminal at Gatwick Airport, 'the Beehive' in 1936 by Hoar, Marlow and Lovett, with its underground tunnel to the railway station, and, later, YRM's design for the new Gatwick Airport in 1955 that integrated road, rail and air for the first time in an interchange under a single roof.

Today's international hub terminals are becoming increasingly large and complex, as the exploded view of the Terminal 5 main building on the following page shows. Add to this the series of satellite buildings and the infrastructure is truly awesome. Again add to this the complex access arrangements by road from the M25, including a major coach and bus station, the extensions of the Heathrow Express and London Underground, together with passengers moving between buildings by the underground transit systems, or transferring from the other existing terminals, and we have not a terminal, but a complex interchange.

Bringing all these routes together is crucial not just to make the act of interchange as speedy as possible, but to ensure the complex is legible to passengers. Simple yet direct passenger routes have the benefit not just of minimising walking time, but maximising the time spent in the lounge areas and retail outlets. Similarly with transfers from one plane to another, the airlines, with their need to reduce minimum connection times and maximise connection opportunities, and the airport, which needs to maximise retail dwell-time, both have a common interest in reducing the transfer time to meet the expectations of the increasingly sophisticated travelling public.

Secondly, environmental concerns mean that airports can no longer consume vast areas of land and have to minimise their impact on the environment and society. For example, Airport de Paris in an annual report proudly shows that Charles de Gaulle Airport occupies land that is the equivalent of a third of the whole of Paris, with further expansion planned. But in many European countries land is one of the scarcest resources. So when expanding an existing airport, if a dedicated short-haul runway is provided with apron areas to suit narrow-bodied aircraft, land take can be radically reduced. The reduction in distances involved also means the aircraft burn less fuel as they taxi on the ground. This idea formed the basis of YRM's concept for a third short

YRM, **Gatwick Airport, South Terminal, 1985.**

YRM **proposal for Heathrow Airport Terminal 5 check-in, due to open in 2008.**

What matters to the traveller is not just an individual experience at a moment in time, but the continuity of experience from the moment of booking a trip, through the journey to the airport, then checking in, to boarding the aircraft and flying out.

runway and Terminal 6 at Heathrow in 2000.

Expanding an airport by adding traffic through an existing facility increases the 'busy hour rate', and hence the landside traffic generation, by less than providing a separate new facility of equivalent size. Therefore, the presumption should always be to expand rather than build on a new site if peak-hour increases in traffic are to be minimised. A move from private to public transport is also required with most of the major improvements being achieved from the introduction of new rail links, as has been successfully demonstrated by the Heathrow Express Rail Link. So, from a surface access point of view, concentrating the interchange between surface and air transport into fewer larger interchange terminals makes sense both in reducing peak traffic levels and in making it possible to invest in a sophisticated public transport network.

This, however, produces significant challenges in mitigating noise nuisance, and in meeting EU air-quality standards. Newer aircraft types are being designed both to reduce noise impact and reduce nitrogen oxide emissions, but with most of the emissions coming from surface traffic rather than aircraft this, too, suggests a move to public transport is inevitable.

Thirdly, the passenger experience in this new type of building is quite different from the way architecture is usually enjoyed. What matters to the traveller is not just an individual experience at a moment in time, but the continuity of experience from the moment of booking a trip, through the journey to the airport, then checking in, to boarding the aircraft and flying out. An airport can be so large it cannot be seen or experienced as a whole. The passenger sees only fragments, as if through blinkers. It is a largely internal experience, marked by stress at critical decision points. YRM recognises that one of the designer's

Richard Rogers, Heathrow Airport Terminal 5. Exploded view by YRM.

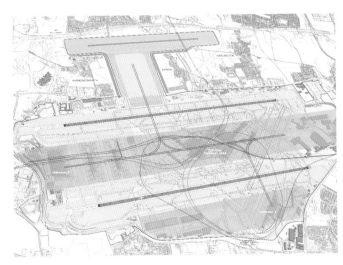

YRM, outline proposal for Heathrow Airport Runway 3 and Terminal 6.

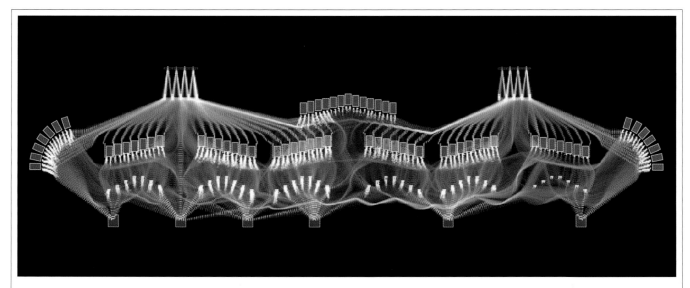

YRM has developed the practice's own pedestrian simulation software, known as Skywalker, which displays and animates the predicted movement of passengers and their response to the environment. The simulation is fully interactive and runs in real time, meaning that assumptions can be altered as the simulation progresses and results can be viewed immediately. This flexibility means that Skywalker is equally suitable as a design tool, a performance predictor, a scenario tester or an on-the-day management tool.

The main drive behind the development of Skywalker was to eliminate the so-called 'black box' approach to simulation. Accordingly, Skywalker is accessible to the client with an understandable interface, fully auditable processes and immediate feedback that visually relates to real-life behaviour.

Each pedestrian in Skywalker is processed individually, with unique characteristics and behaviour generated from a given set of assumptions. This is in contrast to traditional simulations that are generally processed in an 'offline' batch-mode, and deal with raw passenger numbers and group behaviour only, with no means to modify the simulation as time progresses.

Proof of concept has been achieved with a Skywalker model of the check-in concourse at Heathrow's Terminal 5. Current development is focusing on bench-marking and calibration at existing terminals, a comprehensive set of output and input reports, and tighter integration with industry-standard software packages such as AutoCAD. Future plans include continuing innovation of procedures and behaviours that can be represented, such as the use of free time, and the capability to drive YRM's 3-D visualisations.

main tasks is to ease those transitions from one space to another by making the spatial organisation conducive to intuitive way-finding. The ideal is to see the chosen exit from a space as soon as it is entered.

Passengers also require freedom to make choices for themselves. 'E' technology is beginning to change the ways people use terminals, as more and more people elect to check-in 'online' at home and print their own boarding card. So people are arriving at the airport in different states of readiness depending on which operations in the check-in process they have completed off site. At Heathrow's Terminal 5, YRM has introduced a new way of organising the check-in concourse to respond to the 'state of readiness' of the passengers, rather than according to class of travel or destination.

Predicting how people will behave given this level of choice has led YRM to develop its own interactive passenger flow modelling simulation – 'Skywalker' – which allows the user to change inputs while the model is running. Desks can be opened and closed during the working day, transaction times varied, and individual passenger characteristics altered during the simulation. An image of the trails left behind by passengers becomes a work of art in itself, as shown in the almost 'Futurist' image above, with its celebration of speed of movement, which was exhibited at London's Royal Academy Summer Exhibition in 2004.

The places where people will spend their time may change, perhaps with less time in queues and more time in the lounge where they will expect a better retail and leisure offer, now an integral part of the travel experience. But more personal choice inevitably means more complexity. Making large, complex interchange terminals understandable is surely a major challenge for the next generation of airport designers. Airports have become megastructures in that they continually grow and change to meet new business developments, whether the introduction of the A380 aircraft, the growth of retail or the emergence of low-cost airlines, and in an organic way – just like cities. ◬

Notes
1. Reyner Banham, *Megastructure: Urban Futures of the Recent Past*, Thames and Hudson (London), 1976, pp 17–18.
2. FT Marinetti, 'The Founding and Manifesto of Futurism 1909', *Le Figaro*, Paris, 20 February 1909.
3. Umbro Appollonio (ed), *Futurist Manifestos*, Museum of Fine Arts, MFA Publications (Boston, MA), 2001, p 22, translations first published 1973.
4. Reyner Banham, *Theory and Design in the First Machine Age*, Architectural Press (Oxford), 1997, p 127, first published 1960.
5. Antonio Sant'Elia, 'Manifesto of Futurist Architecture', August 1914, in Umbro Appollonio op cit, pp 160–172.

Hollywood's Noir Detours: Unease in the Mental Megalopolis

The Fifth Element (1997).

Hollywood cinema entertained urban audiences, but it also encapsulated their experiences in a paradoxical way. The US film noir cycle, commonly seen as downbeat B-movies made between 1941 and 1958, presented negative counterpoints to the advantages of modern life. **Graham Barnfield** argues that film noir is nothing if not a mental megalopolis, originating a sensibility that continues to underpin cinematic visions of the future in our age of blinding computer-generated imagery (CGI).

Sin City (2005) combined technical brilliance with emotional emptiness. Its 'Basin City' setting was created in post-production, a fake location added in around the actors who performed in front of a green screen. It is a city of the mind, built up through cinematic perceptions of urban life. The stylised film noir of Rodriguez and Miller's comic-book caper is the latest instalment in the artificial tradition of cities made on cleverly lit Hollywood sound stages since the early 1940s.

Where urban life began, urban fictions followed on. Modern public spaces begot modern entertainment. As new entertainments were born, cinema came to the fore. The novelty of projected moving images – 'the cinema of attractions' – was sidelined by content. Narrative and plot, while seldom sophisticated, helped ensure the transition from passing fad to permanent institution. Cinema bedded in well, and later saw off the challenges posed by television and video. Over time, films set in urban localities – even fake ones – acquired a global reach.

Hollywood entertained urban audiences while encapsulating their experiences. It did so in a paradoxical way, often creating a negative counterpoint to modern life. Nowhere was this more apparent than in the cycle of film noir that characterised a fair slice of US film production in the years 1941 to 1958. If film noir is seen as a sensibility – the 'genre' label came later via France – then it established an empire of the imagination throughout cinema and beyond. Film noir is nothing if not a mental megalopolis. Made on Hollywood's poverty row, a picture like *Detour* (1945) embodies noir in microcosm. Director Edgar G Ulmer used minuscule resources, rationed to an estimated 4500 metres (15,000 feet) of film and six days, to come up with the picture. Ann Savage does the business as an alcoholic femme fatale, in a performance matching that of her unsavoury co-star

Tom Neal. Neal opens *Detour* claiming that 'fate or some mysterious force has put the finger on you or me for no good reason at all'. This expresses the sentiment that modern life represents a loss of control, at the heart of the noir sensibility.

Is this outlook uniquely noir? Admittedly, the alienating megalopolis was portrayed brilliantly on the screen in Fritz Lang's *Metropolis* (1926) and Charlie Chaplin's *Modern Times* (1936). Yet after 1940, the connection between cinemas and cities was articulated as a troubled one as a matter of routine. This is not to advocate that Hollywood should produce uplifting tributes to the metropolis, in the manner of Soviet comedies rhapsodising over tractor factories. Moreover, one should not forget that a noir movie was often a B-movie too, the downbeat support act in a double bill shared with such glossy celebrations of urban life as Kelly and Donen's *On the Town* (1949). Whereas big-budget Hollywood celebrated the American way, a morbid melodrama playing support could remind audiences of the dark side of prosperity.

US hard-boiled fiction is noir's literary antecedent. It was as concerned with urban life as with its staple topic – crime – and developed roughly in tandem with Hollywood: hard-boiled mixed pulp publishing, staccato prose and low-life characters. Maturing stylistically with Dashiell Hammett and thematically with a broad range of left-leaning crime writers, hard-boiled was as distinctively American as it was socially critical. Consequently, it became a rich vein of material for Hollywood, from cheap productions like *Raw Deal* (1948) to A-list pictures starring Bogart and Bacall (*The Big Sleep*, *Dark Passage*, *Key Largo*, *To Have and Have Not*). Young adults saw these movies at a time of social dislocation: returning from the war, on shore leave, on a date with a man who could be dead the next

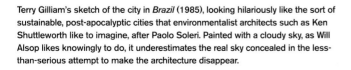

Terry Gilliam's sketch of the city in *Brazil* (1985), looking hilariously like the sort of sustainable, post-apocalyptic cities that environmentalist architects such as Ken Shuttleworth like to imagine, after Paolo Soleri. Painted with a cloudy sky, as Will Alsop likes knowingly to do, it underestimates the real sky concealed in the less-than-serious attempt to make the architecture disappear.

Dark City (1998).

week. Noir's grasp of the cultural moment was reinforced by an explosion in pulp publishing. Reading paperback originals bought at drugstores and malt stands was like seeing the movies all over again. That *Sin City* owes much to Mickey Spillane shows the persistence of this tradition.

Over time, these nightmare themes spread to the suburbs. Movies like *Too Late for Tears* (1949) were part of a cycle of anti-materialist noir spelling out the message that money couldn't buy you happiness. Don Siegel's *Private Hell 36* (1954) transmuted trailer parks into purgatory long before Eminem. Suburban malaise more than matched its urban counterpart. Noir titles – *Caged, Caught, Cornered, Detour, Quicksand, Roadblock, Trapped* – speak to a sense of geographical terminus. The human spirit, constricted within individual characters, finds no salvation in mobility, only new outlets for destructive impulses. The urban/suburban distinction, a source of symbolic mortal combat drawing in US town planners and residents' associations, does not constrain noir cinema. Instead, malaise and exhaustion become the B-movie norm, even as prospects were improving for white-collar white suburbanites, in federally subsidised housing and GI Bill educations. For baby-boom parents, noir reminded them of their misspent youth, the dark side of membership of the 'Greatest Generation'. Increasingly, noir flickered on suburban TV screens late into the night, at odds with new realities, yet still unsettling. As the US noir cycle ground to a halt brilliantly, with Orson Welles' classic *Touch of Evil* (1958), it appeared that the film industry had left its wayward child behind.

Ultimately, this was not a mood restricted exclusively to noir. In tandem with negative literary portrayals of suburbia,

suburbs became an equivalent site of cinematic alienation, from *The Stepford Wives* (1975, 2004) through *Assault on Precinct 13* (1976, 2005) to *The Truman Show* (1998). Sprawl becomes soulless, if not a threat to nature itself. Seen as yet another false utopia, suburbia ducks brickbats from a downbeat sensibility. This is most apparent with the cinematic treatment of Los Angeles, where noir nightmares unfold along an urban-suburban continuum with impunity.

It was not until the mid-1970s that a 'neo-noir' revival was under way, starting with John Cassavetes' *The Killing of a Chinese Bookie* (1976) and ending in Quentin Tarantino's *Reservoir Dogs* (1992). Astute observers noted the similarities between *Dogs* and Ringo Lam's *City on Fire* (1987), in which Hong Kong is rendered as a threatening megalopolis. More broadly, sci-fi spectaculars such as *Blade Runner* (1982) and *The Fifth Element* (1997) routinely, and often inventively, projected traces of the genre into the future. What began as B-movies to keep studio sets and contract players in full

Blade Runner (1982).

Sci-fi spectaculars such as *Blade Runner* (1982) and *The Fifth Element* (1997) routinely, and often inventively, projected traces of the genre into the future. What began as B-movies to keep studio sets and contract players in full employment became a staple feature of modern blockbusters.

employment became a staple feature of modern blockbusters. In tandem, movies set for box-office failure build in noir guarantors of cult status. Thus Tarantino's Los Angeles is awash with profanity, whereas Alex Proyas' titular *Dark City* (1998) may not even exist. The blockbuster and B-movie aspects gelled together with Tim Burton's *Batman* (1989), reworking New York as Gotham once again, and with Christopher Nolan's *Batman Begins* (2005).

The two-way traffic between Hollywood and other national cinemas had interesting consequences for noir. There was a recognised kinship between doomed B-movie protagonists and the black-market figure evolving into the yakuza of postwar Japanese film. While *Stray Dog* (Nora inu, 1949) and *Branded to Kill* (Koroshi no rakuin, 1967) typified this trend, the urban landscape around them evolved into a sleek yet dangerous environment (when left alone by Godzilla). Routinely, this nascent nightmare vision intersected with fantasy, whether underscoring the works of Takashi Miike or the full-blown misanthropy of *Tokyo: The Last Megalopolis* (Teito monogatari, 1999). In animation, the manga genre magnified these trends, to the possibly apocryphal point where Osamu Tezuka's Metropolis (*Metoroporisu*, 2001) was generated when its director heard a plot synopsis of the Lang original. Such trends had already coalesced in *Blade Runner,* embodying a love-hate relationship with all things Japanese.

Sprawling futuristic cities embody contemporary insecurity. Regardless of the technology – in both its fictitious, on-screen form and that employed in film production itself – the Hollywood computer-generated imagery (CGI) megalopolis is usually built on strong noir foundations. Without it, the dystopia demanded by modern misanthropy would stray into Tolkeinian fantasy. Thus, despite central performances from Harrison Ford in both, the gulf between *Star Wars* and *Blade Runner* is there for all to see. While fictional futures appear as grim as the fatalistic prognosis that opens *Detour*, CGI and the green screen frees film-makers from the constraints binding genuine architects. Noir remains an attitude despite technological developments in post-production.

So, two cheers for noir! Let us cherish its critical function and power to unsettle, and its ability to house creative talents. It did both in discreet and explicit ways, and not always in a convincing fashion. Yet over time its critical venom has been drawn. As I argue elsewhere, when 'cable TV leaves Turner Classic Movies chuntering on to itself in the small hours with weekly screenings of *Gaslight* and *The Mask of Dimitrios*, noir's uncanny and explanatory power is not readily apparent'.[1]

The generalisation of the noir sensibility is not so much subversive as a modern repository of self-hatred and pessimism. Viewed as an autonomous cultural product, it holds up a mirror to our dark nights of the soul. But seen as the sole voice expressing our general disenchantment with the megalopolis, it simply reinforces the obstructions to the kind of settlements we need. If noir is everywhere and nowhere today, prepackaged, repackaged and pastiched, it becomes a less than useful factor in the debate over our common future. ⟁

All images courtesy of RotoVision and Matt Hanson, author of *Building Sci-Fi Moviescapes,* RotoVision (Hove), 2005, on www.rotovision.com.

While fictional futures appear as grim as the fatalistic prognosis that opens *Detour*, CGI and the green screen frees film-makers from the constraints binding genuine architects. Noir remains an attitude despite technological developments in post-production.

Note
1. Graham Barnfield, review of Paula Rabinowitz, *Black and White and Noir: America's Pulp Modernism.* Columbia University Press (New York), 2002, in *Historical Materialism* Vol 11.4, 2003, p 420.

Contributor Biographies

Ian Abley has practised widely, currently at YRM Architects, after two years as a senior facade architect at Whitbybird engineers, and three as a site architect for epr architects. His work has tended to be technical, concerned with the detailing and quality of construction. As a counterbalance he has developed the www.audacity.org website since 2000 to collaborate with those who want to better understand the wider social and commercial context for the development sector. He was co-editor, with James Heartfield, of *Sustaining Architecture in the Anti-Machine Age* (Wiley-Academy 2002), a collection of essays variously advocating and critical of sustainability. He followed this with *Why is Construction So Backward?* (Wiley-Academy 2004) and 'Homes 2016', co-authored with James Woudhuysen in 2004.

Jonathan Schwinge was a scholarship diploma student at the AA. His fourth-year diploma project, 'Airlander', was exhibited at Imagination's Ford Journey Zone in the Greenwich Millennium Dome. His final-year project, 'Lost-Exchange', won the Grand Prize and Category Prize for the Bentley Systems Student Design Competition, USA, in 2000. He illustrated both of Ian Abley's earlier books, and it is his sense of architectural style and interest in advanced technology that has inspired this collaborative issue of AD. He currently works part-time at Allies and Morrison architects, and is engaged in his own architectural and product development venture (www.schwinge.co.uk).

Michelle Addington is an associate professor of architecture at Harvard. She is co-author, with Daniel L Schodek, of *Smart Materials and Technologies in Architecture* (Architectural Press, 2004). She is both an architect and an engineer and, originally educated as a nuclear and mechanical engineer, began her career with NASA. After a decade in industry, she studied architecture, and joined a small Philadelphia firm as a project architect. She joined the faculty of Harvard's Graduate School of Design in 1996, where her research focuses on alternative thermal conditioning systems and discrete micro-environments, particularly through the leveraging of advanced technologies and materials.

Graham Barnfield is programme leader in journalism at the University of East London. A Fellow of the Wolfsonian-FIU, he has written widely on US cultural politics and policy in 1930s America. Past journalism has included a film column for *TES Extra: New Teachers*, and contributions to a wide range of publications. He is currently an affiliate editor of *Reconstruction* (www.reconstruction.ws) and *MagLab*. Through his writings on reality TV and documentaries, he has emerged as the main commentator on 'happy slapping' in contemporary Britain.

Pamela Charlick and **Natasha Nicholson** are partners in charlick+nicholson architects. An ecological approach to architecture is a rich source of inspiration and motivation in their work. The practice enjoys working on a varied mix of projects from domestic scale to the master planning of larger sites. Pamela and Natasha have acted as RIBA competition advisers, and have worked as tutors and visiting critics at London Metropolitan and Brighton universities, and at the Architectural Association (AA). Pamela is also a trustee of the charity London 21, which promotes community-based sustainability initiatives. In 2000 charlick+nicholson initiated and curated the 'London Living City' exhibition at the RIBA, which explored urban sustainability issues.

Ceri Dingle and **Viv Regan** are respectively director and assistant director of the education charity, NGO and NVYO WORLDwrite, and the co-directors of the global awareness consultancy ME-WE.

Bee Flowers is a Dutch artist and photographer who has lived in Moscow for the past 15 years. He has a special interest in Russian megastructures, and his photography relating to this subject was recently shown in Moscow. His work has been reviewed in Russia's prestigious daily, *Vedomosti*, a *Wall Street Journal* venture, and is held in private and public collections such as the Moscow Museum of Modern Art. His website (www.beeflowers.com) features an extensive selection of photos of Moscow's modern districts.

Frank Furedi is a professor of sociology at the University of Kent, and author of *Therapy Culture: Cultivating Vulnerability i n an Uncertain Age* (Routledge, 2003) and *Culture of Fear* (Continuum, 2005, first published 1997). Since 1995 his work has focused on the different manifestations of contemporary risk-consciousness. Since 11 September 2001, he has been exploring the way that the reaction to the attack on the World Trade Center provides insights into the contemporary consciousness of risk, and the impact of this episode on the public perception of risk. He is concerned with the cultural influences that have encouraged society to become risk-averse and to feel a heightened sense of vulnerability.

James Heartfield is a director of Audacity Ltd. He writes and lectures on the creative industries, the new economy and the potential of the British construction industry. He co-edited, with Ian Abley, *Sustaining Architecture in the Anti-Machine Age* (Wiley-Academy 2002), and has written for *The Times*, the *Times* Education Supplement, the *Guardian*, *Blueprint* and the *Architects' Journal*. In 1998 he published *Need and Desire in the Post-Material Economy* (Sheffield Hallam University Press), and in 2000 *Great Expectations: The Creative Industries in the New Economy* (Design Agenda). He is currently working on *Let's Build!*, a book about the evident opportunities and policy obstacles facing development in the UK.

Oliver Houchell is a London-based architect with an engineering background who was educated at the Kent Institute of Art and Design in Canterbury, Oxford Brookes University and the AA. He has both studied and worked in practice alongside guest-editor of this issue Jonathan Schwinge, sharing a mutual interest in the architectural applications of technology transfer. He currently works at Wilkinson Eyre Architects. A keen diver, climber and sailor, he likes to combine his passions for technical sports and physiology, both of which inform his professional interest in extreme environmental habitation.

Joe Kaplinsky is a science writer and technology analyst. He has postgraduate training in both physics and mathematics and works as a patent researcher, tracking the novelty and history of inventions. He has written about the need for innovation in the energy industry in *Chemistry and Industry*, and the dangers of holding back nanotechnology in *Science and Public Affairs*.

Stephen Kieran and **James Timberlake** founded KieranTimberlake Associates in Philadelphia in 1984. Their individual academic records are impeccable. They have received 40 design awards in 20 years, including two Gold Medals and two Distinguished Building Awards from the American Institute of Architects (AIA). Both awarded the Rome Prize by the American Academy in Rome prior to setting up their practice, they have also both served as the Eero Saarinen Distinguished Professor of Design at Yale University. They were awarded the inaugural 2001 Benjamin Latrobe Fellowship for architectural design research by the AIA College of Fellows, and were the Max Fisher Chair recipients at the University of Michigan for 2004. They serve as adjunct professors at the University of Pennsylvania's School of Design, where they lead a graduate research studio.

Stanley Mathews is an architect and architectural historian. He received his MArch from Virginia Tech in Blacksburg, Virginia, in 1987, and practised in Cleveland, Ohio, before returning to academia to earn his PhD in architectural history and theory from Columbia University in 2003. He has written for *Dialogue*, *Inland Architect*, the *New Art Examiner* and *Progressive Architecture* magazines. He joined the faculty of Hobart and William Smith Colleges in New York State in 2000, where he teaches architectural history, theory and design. He wrote his doctoral dissertation on Cedric Price's Fun Palace and Potteries Thinkbelt. In the process of researching this work, he became friends with Cedric and convened a memorial symposium at New York's Architectural League to honour Cedric after his death in 2003. He is currently completing a book on Price's early work, to be published in late 2006 by Black Dog Publishing.

John McKean has been an architect, historian and critic, but mainly a teacher, and since 1996 a professor of architecture at the University of Brighton. He has been a regular critic for many years, publishing in *Architectural Design*, the *RIBA Journal*, *Building Design*, *Architectural Review*, *Spazio e Società*, *Places* and *Architèse*, as well as regularly in the *Architects' Journal* (as technical and news editor for some years). He has run architectural and interiors studios in east London, north London and, since 1990, Brighton. Prior to this he taught at the AA, and design history at Middlesex University. His latest book, *Giancarlo De Carlo: Layered Places*, was the text for a Centre Pompidou exhibition on De Carlo's work in the spring of 2004. He has been invited to edit the 21st edition of Banister Fletcher's *History of Architecture*, and is currently considering a radical rethink of the book.

Jayne Merkel is a New York-based contributing editor and member of the editorial board of AD, who formerly edited *Oculus* magazine in New York. She served as the architecture critic of the *Cincinnati Enquirer*, and has written for numerous publications. Her monograph, *Eero Saarinen*, was published by Phaidon Press in September 2004, long after she wrote her master's thesis with Henry-Russell Hitchcock on Eero's father, the celebrated Finnish architect Eliel Saarinen.

Gordon Murray was born in Rottenrow, Glasgow, adjacent to the school of architecture at Strathclyde University, which he entered some 18 years later and to which he returned in 2002 as a visiting professor. He is a principal in gm+ad architects, having practised in Glasgow for 25 years. As an established practice in the city, the firm is recognised for projects across Scotland and, more recently, Europe, which are both thoughtful and provoking. Gordon is president of RIAS, the body representing the profession in Scotland, and also a member of the board of the Lighthouse, Scotland's Centre for Architecture and Design.

Martin Pawley is a writer and critic with a weekly column in the *Architects' Journal*. He studied architecture at the École Nationale Superieure des Beaux-Arts, Paris, and the AA in London. A former editor of the weekly journal *Building Design*, he was later architecture critic for the *Guardian* and the *Observer*, and then editor of the international magazine *World Architecture*. After the seminal *Theory and Design in the Second Machine Age* (Blackwell, 1990), his most recent books have included *Buckminster Fuller: A Critical Biography*, *Future Systems: The Story of Tomorrow* (Phaidon, 2003), *Norman Foster: A Global Architecture* (Universe, 1999) and *20th Century Architecture: A Readers' Guide* (Architectural Press, 1999).

Robert Stewart is the director of YRM Architects, primarily concerned with the development of transport interchanges. He joined YRM in 1981 as project manager for the Gatwick North Terminal Development, and now provides the overall direction for YRM in transportation projects, with particular emphasis on strategic design and master planning. He has led YRM teams through more than 40 transportation projects, including key roles in the integrated British Airways/BAA design team on the Heathrow Terminal 5 project. He was instrumental in the new terminal for Bristol International Airport, and has undertaken work at Birmingham, Cardiff and Swansea airports. He has also led a series of rail and interchange projects, including for Eurostar, Network Rail and London Underground.

Jennifer Taylor is an architect and writer primarily known for her publications on Australian and Japanese architecture. She graduated (BArch, 1967, and MArch, 1969) from the University of Washington, Seattle, and has since taught in many architectural schools throughout the world. She is currently at the Queensland University of Technology. She was awarded the Japan Foundation Fellowship in 1975 and in 1994/5. In 1998 she was honoured with the inaugural RAIA Marion Mahony Griffin Award for writing and teaching, and in 2000 with the inaugural RAIA National Education Prize. She received the UIA Jean Tschumi Prize honourable mention for architectural criticism and architectural education in 1999.

theboxtank is Corey Hoelker, Emily Andersen and Geoff DeOld, all of whom live and work in New York City. theboxtank is a collaborative focused on the relation between retail, urbanism and infrastructure. www.theboxtank.com is a weblog about big-box urbanism, a major force behind the development and culture of the contemporary American city. Its emphasis is retailing giant Wal-Mart. **Corey Hoelker** studied architecture at the University of Nebraska-Lincoln, and received his master of architecture from Columbia. He is currently a designer at Rogers Marvel Architects in New York. **Emily Andersen** earned her master of architecture from the University of Nebraska-Lincoln, before spending time at Thanhauser Esterson & Kappel in New York City, then moving to Slade Architecture where she is a designer. **Geoff DeOld** received his master of architecture from the University of Nebraska-Lincoln. He spent a year at Randy Brown Architects in Omaha and is currently with STUDIOS Architecture in New York City.

James Woudhuysen is professor of forecasting and innovation at De Montfort University, Leicester, and is on the board of the Department of Trade & Industry's Housing Forum. He graduated in physics, then edited *Design* magazine, and co-founded *Blueprint*. He was head of research at international designers Fitch, before moving to the Henley Centre, then Philips Consumer Electronics (the Netherlands). From 1997 to 2001 he was a director of product designers Seymour Powell. A director of Audacity Ltd, he co-wrote, with Ian Abley, *Why is Construction So Backward?* and *Homes 2016*. He also completed *The Globalisation of UK Manufacturing and Services 2004–24* for the government. AD

Contents ⚠+

110+

122+

⚠+

125+

McLaren Technology Centre

The product of a highly customised production process, the racing car is the very antithesis of the modular and the mass produced. **Jeremy Melvin** reveals how Foster and Partners has designed a headquarters for the McLaren Group – a premier producer and promoter of Formula One cars – that, despite its location on the site of an old farm in Woking, Surrey, is resplendent as a 'late industrial vision of the object perfectly refined to fulfil its allotted task'.

Foster and Partners, McLaren headquarters, Woking, Surrey, 2005
The new building started with a wind tunnel, providing McLaren with its own
facility for the first time.

'Ninety per cent NASA, ten per cent Disney', David Nelson and Nigel Dauncey from Foster and Partners remember McLaren boss Ron Dennis adding to their design brief.

The affinity with NASA is obvious. Throughout the ground floor and several basement levels, black-clad workers test and assemble cars with all the care that one might hope the space agency takes over its rockets. The bays for examining the Formula One cars when they return to the factory between races are closer to an operating theatre than the usual grime-coated inspection pit of a local garage. Even the assembly line for the road-going Mercedes-Benz SLR, which McLaren designs and produces for its 40 per cent shareholder and engine supplier Daimler Chrysler, and where these third-of-a-million pound toys are nursed into existence at the rate of three a day, has something of a hospital about it. On the upper floor are offices, and in one of them McLaren Applied Technologies, a division of the company set up to find and exploit potential spin-offs for ideas developed for racing cars, conceived components for the *Mars Lander.*

Only in the unlikely context of the basement does the element of Disney become apparent. Running through it is a large passage that connects to all the main spaces above. At Disneyland, such a device means that the public have the benefit of modern servicing without the outside world intruding into the fantasy. For McLaren the effect is almost the reverse. Here *deus ex machina* becomes *machina ex dei*, as the highest technology springs fully formed from the ground as if born from the earth itself.

The essence of McLaren's business is orchestrating spectacle, whether on the racetrack or luring sponsors and purchasers into its building. Even employees are subject to a similar system. On leaving their cars they enter the building via glass pavilions, which take them under the service yard into a network that distributes them to their allotted work places. Like Disney, the spectacle nurtures the brand. It is no coincidence that an as yet unused part of the building – tucked away underground and still unfitted – was designed to become a visitor experience centre, and another of the company's five divisions, McLaren Marketing, is devoted to finding benefits for their sponsors who pay royally for their association with one of Formula One's most successful teams.

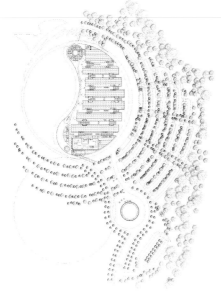

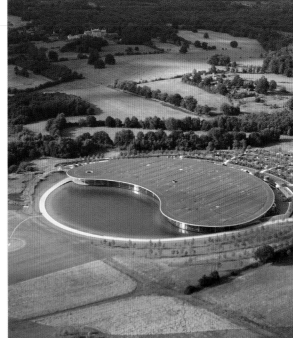

The building and lake form a circle within a landscaped park.

So this is a building and a business where aesthetics is essential. It is not, of course, aesthetics in the sense that Sir Ernst Gombrich or Aby Warburg used the term. Rather, it is that late industrial vision of the object perfectly refined to fulfil its allotted task, where functional pleasure and aesthetic satisfaction are seen as co-terminal. All architects have to have an eye on their clients' requirements, but in this instance architect and client share not just a vision, but a modus operandi – and in the case of Ron Dennis and Norman Foster, a birthday too.

Like many successful organisations, from the House of Commons to Vodafone, McLaren rose to prominence despite, rather than because of, the architectural quality of its premises. Its operations were spread over several sites around Woking and, from the moment Dennis bought the company in 1980, he had the ambition of bringing them all together on one site. It took him until the mid-1990s to do so.

McLaren looked at several locations, including one as far away from its base as Dover, but its highly skilled employees vetoed that. Instead, it bought a 56-hectare (138-acre) farm just outside Woking, which had a series of farm buildings more or less in the centre and where the district and county councils were keen to keep a provider of a thousand jobs for the area. Nelson explains that the building footprint is more or less the same as what it replaces, and some subtle landscape manipulation, reusing soil rather than taking it off site, adds to the concealment. Even so, there was a strict height limit.

The design began to take shape within these basic parameters. The landscape plays a vital part, creating a sense of surprise and delight for visitors when the building is finally revealed, viewed from the approach road across a lake. Even the water combines aesthetics and function. It reflects sunlight into the interior, and also helps with the cooling load, especially from the wind tunnel where car aerodynamics are tested and refined. In a curious analogue, the lake's shape derives of the natural movement of fluid dynamics, which assists circulation of water and the heat it carries, significantly reducing the need for mechanical pumping in recycling that energy. Functional affinities extend into the invisible.

The wind tunnel was one of the prime motivations behind the new building. Previously McLaren hired a facility and Dennis was keen to acquire his own, as the ability to continue development right up to the last minute is essential to being competitive. It was installed and running while the rest of the building took shape around it, but the same ethos informed the entire design.

The staff restaurant overlooks the lake.

View of the boulevard with triumphant cars of the past. The horizontal fins on the glass were designed in conjunction with McLaren engineers.

Nelson explains that with the envelope more or less fixed by planning restrictions, Fosters had to find an alternative to providing flexibility to the standard industrial solution of an extrudable section. Instead, the building breaks down into five 18-metre (60-foot) wide fingers, separated by passages wide enough to serve as means of escape, and a certain amount of storage.

After much balancing of flexibility against cost, it was decided to give these fingers a clear span of 12 metres (40 feet). On the ground level they are largely assembly areas, one being the SLR production line, with others devoted to Formula One cars. Here, at any point in the design, the precise needs were liable to change, as a new and more sophisticated machine-tool testing device, capable of knocking a fraction or two of a second off lap times, might have become available. This was functional design where the precise function was not always known. While the main structure may be unalterable, the services installation is easily accessible and could be replaced.

Above the assembly shops are the offices, each approached via a circular 'pod' reached from a narrow, elevated walkway that is hung from the roof and snakes its way across the boulevard that overlooks the lake. In such a deep-plan building, providing daylight might have been difficult, but working with Targetti and McLaren, Fosters designed a neat lighting system that combines natural and artificial light. Recognisably coming from the Foster stable, but with an added attention to visual detail that comes from Dennis, the work places, whether an assembly line or office, exude a precise discipline that belies the intense intellectual effort that goes into the tasks.

All this makes for a great sense of spectacle. The visitor's approach gradually unveils the building and ends at the entrance, under boardroom and corporate offices but leading on to the lakeside boulevard that itself terminates in the restaurant. The odd fish leaps up, and an occasional swan goes for a swim, but nature is as nothing to the technological toys on display.

Whether the purpose of a visit to the centre is to pick up your SLR, or hand over a sum of many magnitudes greater as an F1 sponsor, you see the company's history in its products. The fastest production road-car, cars that have won 11 constructors championships and taken eight drivers to individual glory, are laid out in front of you. Or you might go straight to an extraordinary, circular room where a car in your corporate colours might be shown to you to tempt you into sponsorship. Here technology is turned into spectacle – and it might even be turned into something of quotidian use. ∆+

McGauran Giannini Soon Architects

Shelley Penn describes how a Melbourne-based practice's aspirations for integrity and authenticity have led it away from the usual pursuit of an identifiable visual language and style above content.

I read *The Fountainhead* by Ayn Rand more than 20 years ago, and saw the film soon after. My response was a mixture of hilarity at Howard Roark's absurdly inflated ego, and an almost guilty admiration for the focus, tenacity and transcendent passion he showed in the pursuit of his art.

According to some studies of her work, Rand's central thesis was that greatness and arrogance are inextricably bound together. This idea was ridiculous to me, but was reinforced throughout my architectural education by the unconditional worship of figures such as Le Corbusier and Frank Lloyd Wright, and artists such as Pollock and Picasso.

My view was that it was possible to be a great architect and a decent person.

I went so far as to dismiss architects like Wright because of his selfish treatment of others, and to some extent I felt quite justified in thinking he was overrated. However, this idea came unstuck when I first visited one of his buildings, not long after reading Rand: not one of his best-known works, it was the first building to bring me to tears, and one of my most profound experiences of architecture.

I had to accept that some brilliant architects were also arrogant twerps, but remained hopeful that an enlarged sense of self was not a prerequisite for success.

Twenty years later, I know you don't have to be conceited to be good, and also that great works of architecture are

McGauran Giannini Soon Architects, St Leger Residence, Breamlea, Victoria, Australia, 1999

much more than mere ideas or good looks. But ego and image still seem to be at the core of how we judge and celebrate architecture. Individualism is stronger than ever in all aspects of Western society, and in architecture we tend to align the apparent strength of personality with the quality of the work.

In Australia, many architects aspire to the international hero status of characters like Wright, a desire perhaps more intense given our relatively remote, postcolonial condition. The media searches relentlessly for new celebrities and focuses on the visual show of architecture, again aligning architecture-as-display with architect-as-idol. Related to this in a circular fashion is the truth that many clients believe

temper tantrums, grandstanding, and other genius-like behaviour are signs of a superior artist.

Within the Australian context, Melbourne architects bear an additional collective conceit in their reputation for more intellectually rigorous, avant-garde architecture. The most talked-about practices are the most vocal, and are known for the strong personalities who direct them. Typically, each is recognised by a 'house style' that is the result of either an authentic pursuit of certain themes, or the more superficial application of a didactic or overtly 'original' aesthetic. Their work, which is the most publicised and prominent, is generally thought of as the 'best', and they will probably go down in history

as the best of the time because of how history is recorded, even though the work is often far from great.

Of course, there are several practices that are less well known, but highly respected for their sophisticated work. They're usually less interested in self-promotion, although their work is often better than that produced by 'the names'. On the whole, however, they still tend to fit within the framework of the architect and his or her idiosyncratic oeuvre.

In this context, McGauran Giannini Soon (MGS) is quite a rare thing: an architectural practice not based on image, whose work and bearing show you can be great without being egocentric, and successful in design

McGauran Giannini Soon Architects, St Leger Residence, Breamlea, Victoria, Australia, 1999
This beach house illustrates the strategy of creating two forms that provide a dialogue and framework for response to the varying programmatic and site conditions. Sited on a sand-dune ridge, the house is

flanked by an ocean beach to the south, and low-lying marshlands to the north. Conceived as two elements that appear to slip past one another, the building addresses these two aspects while allowing for projected developments in how the house will be used: from holiday house to future permanent home.

While one form is for active, living spaces that face morning sun and views, and – clad and framed in timber – is open and light in expression, its counterpart is massive and closed, constructed from concrete block, and houses the private, quiet spaces for ablution and rest.

terms without being petulant. The practice is widely published nationally and overseas, and has won numerous awards, but these achievements seem quieter – less about glamour or iterations of house style than about individual projects of merit. Their work does not make a show of being 'original', but it is truly authentic, and the product of integrity and passion. Above all, its directors are decent, congenial individuals who prioritise relationship over personal vision.

Rob McGauran and Mun Soon established the practice in 1985, extending their close friendship from their university days. They were joined not long after by Eli Giannini, Rob's sister-in-law, and most recently by Eli's husband Chris Jones. Over 20 years, they have developed a substantial body of work traversing a range of project types and scales. Although well known for their design work, and for their individual and collective contributions to architecture and the built environment, they have not developed a clear house style. What they consistently demonstrate in all of their endeavours is more of a 'house attitude' – an ongoing concern with relationship and context, and an aversion for wilful, gratuitous gesture. The ego is still strong, but it seems the desire to change the world is based on a broader view than that of most architects.

They say: 'We see a need for architects to engage with the issues of social, economical and environmental sustainability holistically and to use design and advocacy skills to effectively propose changes to this paradigm. Our work to date has given us heart that architects can make a measurable difference to the way our cities and communities develop; that in a world that is increasingly self-centred, there remains potential for collective, compassionate and creative aspirations to be defined, expressed and implemented in our cities, in partnership with the public and private sector, that together enrich and sustain our built environment and the communities that occupy it.'

While many architects would agree, there are very few whose actions fit their rhetoric. Projects completed by MGS include everything from retail and fit-out works, houses, large-scale residential developments, institutional, commercial and industrial projects, as well as master planning and urban designs at major civic scales. The office consists of the four directors, 25 architects or graduates, and five support staff.

McGauran Giannini Soon Architects, Icon restaurant buildings, New Quay, Docklands, Melbourne, Victoria, Australia, 2003
The architectural concept here is clearly articulated and developed. Sited on the edge of a large-scale pedestrian promenade in Melbourne's recently regenerated docklands precinct, the small buildings mediate between a bank of multistorey residential towers and Victoria Harbour. The tactic of inserting sculptural objects that in their formal scale and shape evoke ships, while responding to pedestrian scale and sensibility in material and fine detail, is masterful. This is an example of MGS's intelligent and broad-minded approach to architecture. The concept of creating sculptural objects answers both their interest in building-as-object and the responsibility for how the buildings impact on the greater context in human terms. The buildings transform the promenade and provide it with a scale, focus and beauty previously lacking in the site.

Within this framework, the approach is democratic. Each project is appointed a project architect who is encouraged to conceive, develop and realise the design, with directorial input at concept stage and support throughout the process. The directors neither dictate on design direction nor abrogate responsibility. They are committed to excellence in design, so will step in if things are going off the rails, but aim to respect the project architect's work. What they do give up through this approach is the idea of a particular MGS look, and to some extent they lose the coherence of a singular preoccupation or vision that comes through when a body of work is developed by the one 'hand' – a loss that is great in the context of the architect-as-hero, but almost irrelevant otherwise.

Their commitment to people is carried through to dealings with clients, consultants, builders and, indeed, communities. They are highly successful and increasingly sought-after for community-sensitive projects. A good dose of compassion and an understanding of community concerns means they are capable of effective communication with such groups. But it is more than that. MGS actually care deeply about the impact of architecture and urban design on peoples' lives.

There are very few architects who will allow a 'vision' to shift significantly in response to community concerns while fighting for a strong design outcome at the same time. They tend to either draft up a community/committee-made solution with a weak shrug of relief, or stand fast to the mighty vision and lose, or win by sheer eloquence or force of opinion. In their dealings with communities and councils in this forum, MGS give a great deal in terms of urban design advocacy by demonstrating alternative approaches to resolution and positive outcomes for public projects.

In truth I suspect there's a tension in this practice between the desire to self-express through design in the traditional way, and an awareness of the bigger picture and genuine commitment to improving the human condition. This is evident to some extent in the differences between their houses and the public projects. The houses are more pure architectural studies and it is in these that an interest in certain architectural themes to do with form, space and language is revealed.

There is a consistency in their approach, with most of the houses being ordered by two key elements that define function and create a formal dialogue that is then played out through material

McGauran Giannini Soon Architects, Middle Brighton Baths, Brighton, Victoria, Australia, 2002
In the context of a highly sensitive community, the architects have negotiated a heritage intervention through the process and architectural response in order to achieve a high-quality outcome. New work is contemporary, light and open in contrast to the more closed masonry form of the prewar Art Deco building. The approach to the complex is pedestrian friendly, while at the same time accommodating the requirement for a large car park; and by locating a café in a sunny spot adjacent to the entry, the whole context is enlivened and made vibrant. Port Philip Bay and the sea baths are revealed on entering the building. Internal café spaces open and extend into a promenade overlooking the water, providing views and surveillance of the baths area that would otherwise be visually isolated.

and expression: mass versus frame, solid versus void, and dark versus light. The formal strategy also allows for development of intermediate spaces – either internal or external – that respond dynamically to site and orientation. MGS take obvious pleasure in material, and their work is finely detailed. There is frequently a key detail that is developed to accentuate the beauty of a particular material, and which demonstrates an interest in craft and the richness it brings to experience.

These themes recur in the public projects, but the more broadly human aspects are prioritised – particularly the response to context, and relationships within and around sites. In architectural terms, MGS frequently experiment with or challenge 'type'. For example, in their Focus factory, offices and showroom in Braeside, an industrial project, the usual and economical precast-concrete box form is altered dramatically by cutting circular volumes into and out of it. In their public housing for Woodstock Street Balaclava, a development currently under construction, the form visually mediates between two immediately adjacent types. Using the warehouse 'box' as a base, the form is then lopped by exaggerated 'pitched roof' elements that refer to the archetypal house, again drawing on, but undermining, the type.

Another example is the Gisborne Central Neighbourhood Shopping Centre, a recently completed retail development in regional Victoria. Apart from particular themes explored in the architecture, the public space around the building has been carefully designed to integrate it with an adjacent swimming complex, and the building designed to utilise 40 per cent less energy than its retail counterparts. By negotiating this middle ground, a safe, pedestrian-friendly, civic space has been created and an environmental agenda established – an approach that typifies the MGS interest in a broader social agenda, and the way they respect, address and proactively contribute to the public realm.

I see this as an ideological, or even political, stance, which is further

McGauran Giannini Soon Architects, Mixed Retail and Residential Development, Bay Street, Port Melbourne, Victoria, Australia, 2001
Through the creation of private balconies at first-floor level overlooking busy inner-suburban Bay Street, this project responds to a heritage streetscape by both respecting and stimulating it. A safe environment is provided in the back alley by creating active spaces and an idiosyncratic character that contributes to a sense of community ownership for the residents.

demonstrated in the directors' active engagement with the profession, education and government. Eli Giannini recently completed a term as president of the Victorian Chapter of the Royal Australian Institute of Architects where she lobbied to improve the connection between state government and the design professions with the aim of promoting and protecting good design in public projects and government contracts.

Both Giannini and McGauran have contributed over many years to education at the three major schools of architecture in Victoria. McGauran has served in numerous roles as adviser to state and local government on urban design issues and policy documents, and the practice is in increasing demand for its urban design expertise. This work is clearly not about image – it is largely invisible – however, it contributes enormously to the processes and policies that impact on the built environment in the state.

Despite their very evident commitment to beauty and ideas, I believe McGauran Giannini Soon are ultimately more interested in architecture and urban design as organic reflections of the complexity of the human condition. Rather than seeking to brand themselves through an idiosyncratic language or through their public personas, the directors subvert their respective egos in favour of humanity. In contrast to Ayn Rand's thesis on greatness, they demonstrate that humility in the architect's approach to process, people and design can produce exceptional work.

The degree to which this practice is sought after also perhaps indicates that many people indeed value a less image-based, more holistic approach and a deeper awareness of the big picture – and that Howard Roark might be looking more absurd than ever. ⌂+

Shelley Penn was recently appointed Victoria's first Associate State Government Architect. In addition to this role, she continues to provide independent urban design advice on a number of large-scale public projects while sustaining her solo practice, which is focused on residential architecture. She also maintains an ongoing involvement in architectural education and writing.

Resumé
McGauran Giannini Soon
Architects

2005–06
Public housing, Woodstock Street, Balaclava, Victoria

2005
RAIA Award for Sustainable Architecture: Gisborne Retail Centre, Victoria

Helen Lempriere Sculpture Award (shortlisted): Introduced Spaces (by Sue Buchanan and Eli Giannini), Werribee Park, Werribee, Victoria

Yering Station Sculpture Exhibition and Awards (second prize): Sure2Grow (by Sue Buchanan and Eli Giannini), Yarra Valley, Victoria

2004
Work included in 'Convergent Design' exhibition, Melbourne Hotspots Pavilion, Architectural Biennial Beijing

Work included in 'Melbourne Masters Architecture' exhibition, TarraWarra Museum of Art, Yarra Valley, Victoria

Chris Jones joins MGS as director

2003
RAIA Osborne McCutcheon Award for Commercial Architecture: Icon restaurant buildings, New Quay, Docklands, Melbourne

McGauran Soon changes name to McGauran Giannini Soon (MGS Architects)

2002
Middle Brighton Baths, Brighton, Victoria

2001–04
'Caravaggio in 3D' exhibition, curated by Rob McGauran and Roger Byrt, at the Monash University Art Gallery, Caulfield, Victoria; Broken Hill Regional Gallery, New South Wales; Gosford Regional Art Gallery, New South Wales; Wollongong City Gallery, New South Wales; Riddoch Art Gallery, Mount Gambier, South Australia; Grafton Regional Art Gallery, New South Wales

2001
Mixed retail and residential development, Bay Street, Port Melbourne

RAIA Sisalation Award for Urban Solutions: Propositions for the Future Australian City

2000
Potter Foundation Award (Rob McGauran and Roger Byrt): 'Caravaggio – Distortions in 3D'

1999
RAIA Award for New Residential Architecture: St Leger Residence, Breamlea, Victoria

1998
'Federation Square' exhibition, selected competition entries, 230 Collins Street Gallery, Melbourne

Royal Australian Planning Institute Award: Hoffmans Brickworks – Preparation of Development Guidelines. Guidelines and practice notes for the redevelopment of the historic Hoffmans Brickworks site, Brunswick, Victoria

1997
Design Institute of Australia Interior Design Award: 'Tea', Tea Corporation shop, Chadstone Shopping Centre, Victoria

Eli Giannini made director of MGS

1996
'Metroscape Propositions for the Freeway Environment', curated by Eli Giannini, RMIT Gallery, Storey Hall, Melbourne

RAIA Award of Commendation, Institutional Category: New sailing facilities, Aquatic Drive, Albert Park, Victoria

1995
RAIA Award of Commendation: Peebles Residence, Point Lonsdale, Victoria

BHP 'Steel Futures' Award: Peebles Residence

Eli Giannini receives grant from Australian Council for the Arts (CAED Programme) for Freeway Project

1992
RAIA Award of Excellence, Multiple Residential Category: 9–11 Elwood Street, Brighton, Victoria

1991
RAIA Age Award for House of the Year: Jan Juc House, Victoria

1989
Eli Giannini joins McGauran Soon

1985
McGauran Soon Pty Ltd Architects founded by Rob McGauran and Mun Soon

McLean's Nuggets

Multimodal?
We're All Multimodal Now

Statistics from the recent Department for Transport (DfT) *Transport Trends: 2004 Edition* do not confirm that we are all cycling and walking around 21st-century Britain, but that over the last 20 years these bipedal activities have been in gradual decline with only a little recent recovery. Car use has continued to grow despite all uneven physical and strategic monetary measures. Domestic air travel has increased threefold in the same period by way of competitive pricing in comparison with the privatised rail network's 40 per cent rise in usage with increased prices of 36 per cent in real terms since 1980. There must, however, be doubts that this airborne fuel-intensive local transport network has a long-term future, with large-scale alternatively fuelled aeroplanes not due to arrive any time soon. On 31 December 2002, Shanghai officially launched its maglev rail link from central Shanghai to Pudong International airport, described in Neil Parkyn's excellent book *SuperStructures*. The launch of this 30-kilometre (19-mile) showpiece built by Siemens and ThyssenKrupp was patriotically patronised by the German Chancellor with a view to future and lengthier uses of this magnetic levitation rail system. The success of the new Shanghai link, which recently transported its two-millionth passenger at speeds of 430 kilometres (270 miles) per hour, has led to the formation of transport consortium UK Ultraspeed. Ultraspeed is a proposal for a dedicated UK North–South link reducing current travel times between London and Glasgow on the 'innovative' tilting trains from a 1980s equalling 4 hours and 45 minutes to a genuinely fast 2 hours and 40 minutes. The big concern is cost, although compared with the piecemeal upgrades on the existing West Coast mainline, which have taken 10 years and an estimated £10 billion, one wonders. Multimodal, however, must be the future. London's only tram system (at present) serving Wimbledon to Croydon via Mitcham Junction looks like a train with extremely local stops. Crucially, though, its tram designation does away with bridges and platforms become indiscernible ramps. The once-derided Docklands Light Railway in London has now been extended four times and, despite the accident of 1999 during refurbishment, Wuppertal's over-river monorail continues to serve the German city. It is the inspiration for countless other suspended urban transit technologies – of historical interest, currently operating or under active development – listed on the University of Washington's Innovative Transportation Technologies website. What next? The DfT and the Office of the Deputy Prime Minister have started to promote the possibilities of freight delivery via the UK's excellent and compellingly slow 5100 kilometres (3170 miles) of fully navigable waterways. Parisians get used to new high-speed travelators (operating at a Paris-bus-equalling speed of 9 kilometres (5.5 miles) per hour) and arrivals at St Pancras station, the new home of the Channel Tunnel Rail Link scheduled to open in 2007, will have to get used to the steepest (12°) travelators approved for use by Her Majesty's Rail Inspectorate. Why exclude the use of high-speed people movers such as rollercoasters? In the case of Kingda Ka in New Jersey, US, speeds can reach a nerve-jangling 205 kilometres (127 miles) per hour. Or there's the more sedate Steel Dragon in Japan, which travels at 150 kilometres (93 miles) per hour over the not inconsiderable distance of 2.5 kilometres (1.5 miles), or Big Ben to Marble Arch, in one minute. Add to this news that the Civil Aviation Authority has recently granted a seaplane landing licence for a west coast of Scotland air shuttle operating out of Glasgow's river Clyde, Cardiff Bay's much heralded driverless taxi-cab system ULTra (expected 2007), an elevated cycleway system for the treacherous London street junction, and English Welsh & Scottish Railway Ltd's prototypical sleeping, meeting and working Company Train (recently completed at EWS's Toton works in Nottingham) – all of which reflect a proliferation of mobility providers and an increasingly pluralistic approach to the (predominantly) horizontal transportation business. These may not be mass-transport systems, but as a combined whole should support and stimulate new methods of movement and patterns of work. It is about the journey, it may be about getting there, and it is all about mobility of the multimodal kind.

The 11.23 to South Promenade – hold on tight.

Treading Carefully: Watching Your Ecological Footprints

The World Wildlife Fund defines the Ecological Footprint 'as a measure of how much biologically productive land and water area an individual, a city, a country, a region, or humanity requires to produce the resources it consumes and to absorb the waste it generates'. Devised in 1994 by Mathis Wackernagel and William Rees, and published in their book *Our Ecological Footprint: Reducing Human Impact on the Earth*, this new method of environmental assessment rates our specific impact in global hectares (gha). There are currently an estimated 11.3 billion global hectares of biologically productive land and sea (a quarter of the earth's surface), which aggregated across the current population of the world averages approximately 1.8 gha per person. These footprinting techniques tell us that a US citizen demands a heavyweight 9.6 gha, whilst Indian citizens a more modest 1 gha. The value of such methodology seems to be the useful visualisation of environmental data and an awareness of the synergetic relationship between energy, waste and emissions, production and requisite resources. The problem with such a formula is that, like Hendrik Van Loon's extraordinary statistic from the 1930s that you could fit the whole of the world's population standing up on the Isle of Wight, its informational quality is benign curiosity. In a recent report from the Sustainable Development Unit of Cardiff Council and Cardiff University, published in *eg* magazine, a more specifically useful local analysis is made of Cardiff City's ecological footprint, from food processing to the ecological footprint of a football match at its Millennium Stadium. Ecological parsimony is not enough – it might feel good, but it does not do any. It is important to remember Buckminster Fuller's anti-entropic 'doing more with less' reflects a mental and not merely physical approach to beneficial change.

Evaporative Cooling

Evaporative cooling is the cooling effect stimulated by the adiabatic evaporation of water. When we perspire and our sweat dries this local evaporation cools our body. The unglazed clay of terracotta pots and pipes enables this process through its material porosity, which slowly leaks water. As this water reaches the outer surface of the material, a degree of evaporation occurs, depending on the exterior temperature, causing a cooling effect on the liquid inside. This centuries-old process is effective with a terracotta pot cooling water by as much as 12 to 15 degrees below ambient temperatures. The technology of evaporative cooling is also used in 'swamp coolers' or evaporative air-conditioning, which by blowing air across a water-soaked pad or screen, cool the air by raising humidity. As such these environmentally benign air coolers operate most efficiently in a dry climate (low humidity). It is estimated that there are more than 20 million residential evaporative coolers currently in use, with over a million new units annually fabricated in India. Robert E Foster of New Mexico State University estimates that the operation of these EAC units, in contrast to equivalent 'air conditioning', saves 60 million barrels of oil per annum and 12 million tonnes of associated CO_2 emissions. EAC requires little power other than for the air-moving fan unit, but does require water. In a reversal of this technology, *Leonardo* magazine recently reported a water-harvesting project entitled 'Moisture' by a group of Los Angeles-based artists. Working in the Mojave Desert, artist Adam Belt constructed the Yearning Bush, a facsimile shrub made from copper tube, a refrigerator compressor, solar panel and battery, which operates as a deconstructed dehumidifier. During the day, a solar cell would charge the battery, and before sunrise the refrigerator compressor activates, forming frost on the cool copper tubes (branches).

Portable dehumidifier + cold drink.

When an inbuilt timer shuts off the compressor, the ice melts and droplets of water fall from the bush. All water is 'captured' from the latent moisture in the air in the same way that condensation forms on a bottle of beer 'so ruddy cold there's a sort of dew on the outside of the glass' (actor John Mills dreaming of a cool refreshment in the film *Ice Cold in Alex,* 1958). ⚏+

'McLean's Nuggets' is an ongoing technical series inspired by Will McLean and Samantha Hardingham's enthusiasm for back issues of ⚏, as explicitly explored in Hardingham's ⚏ issue *The 1970s is Here and Now* (March/April 2005). Will McLean is joint coordinator of technical studies in the Department of Architecture at the University of Westminster with Pete Silver. Together they have recently completed a new book entitled *Fabrication: The Designer's Guide* (Elsevier, 2006).

Evelyn Road, Silvertown
Niall McLaughlin Architects

Bruce Stewart describes how the industrial landscape of Silvertown in east London became a design generator for a housing scheme, which benefits from a treatment that is particular to its site and, in so doing, adds to the fabric of the area.

Whilst not within the immediate catchment area for the Thames Gateway redevelopment proposals, the affordable housing at Evelyn Road, Silvertown, in east London, by Niall McLaughlin Architects, has had to overcome many of the problems of that massive rejuvenation of both banks of the Thames Estuary. Completed in 2004, the development of 12 flats for sale under co-ownership was originally a huge postindustrial landscape of decaying and derelict factories, warehouses and docks.

The finished project was the result of a limited competition, 'Fresh Ideas for Low Cost Housing', held by the Peabody Trust, and set up to find young, innovative architectural practices that could take on the challenge of a very demanding site and produce high-quality affordable housing. The initial idea behind the competition was to engage with these firms and select a winner who would then take on the design for three small sites in the Silvertown area. However, it was always the intention that all of those invited to participate would be considered for future work with the Trust.

As it turned out, the standard of the entries was so high that a single winner could not be selected, and two firms, Ash Sakula and Niall McLaughlin, were each given a site to work on (the ground conditions at the third site were such that development there was abandoned).

Niall McLaughlin Architects was founded in 1991 and, over the years, has won several prizes for its work, including 'UK Young Architect of the Year' in 1998. One of the critical starting points in any design, for McLaughlin himself, is the history of the site, the traces and echoes that have led to its present-day condition. This may not have an explicit manifestation in the finished building, but it is a very forceful design generator.

At Silvertown the history of the site is incredibly rich in terms of the development of urban industrial landscapes. From the mid-19th-century industrial boom to the collapse of British manufacturing, there has been immense development and decline, all of which have left traces, both visible and unseen. The range of industrial processes that flowered here was particularly wide: a rubber processing plant (owned by Stephen Winkworth Silver, who gave his name to the area), a Tate and Lyle sugar refinery, munitions, jam, soap, matches. Such processes have left their marks and stains, not least of which is a legacy of contaminated land and the possibility of unexploded ordnance. In addition, poor-

Niall McLaughlin Architects, Everlyn Road low-cost housing, Silvertown, London, 2004
The views out of the site, towards Canary Wharf, for example, were one of the key features the architect wanted to capitalise upon. Windows at all the corners maximise the views of the postindustrial landscape.

quality workers' housing previously stood between the factories on the river frontage and the warehouses on the side of Royal Victoria Dock, so there was also an imprint of the domestic amongst this engine of the empire.

The current condition of the site is one of redevelopment, with an airport, hotel, conference centre and the Britannia village by Barratt Homes already completed. In general, the architectural merit of these new interventions is not high, with the Barratt housing of a very similar design language to its countless suburban developments around the country. However, this is not suburbia, and as such the use of an 'everyplace' idiom is undervaluing the potential of the site for both the residents and the city.

It is against this backdrop that Niall McLaughlin has inserted a very confident, well-resolved scheme. Four main strands of thought guided the design: '1) A rational layout of the interior, with a large, flexible living space; 2) The view from the building, over the strange landscape of London Docklands: London City Airport, Canary Wharf and the Millennium Dome; 3) The strange chemical history of the site; and 4) The nature of modern industrialised construction, in which a timber frame is wrapped in a decorative outer layer.'[1]

At first glance there is very little to connect the Peabody Trust housing to its neighbours, but the construction is similar in both – timber frames clad in 'decorative' skins. However, it is not just choice of cladding that really separates McLaughlin's project from the rest of the recently completed housing in the area. One of the critical factors in providing affordable homes is keeping construction costs as low as reasonably possible, hence the use of basic construction technologies. The key to the success of using basic building methods is in the thinking about the use of the finished home – how it will be lived in.

To maximise one of the explicit features of the site, that it is south

The very distinctive iridescent film used on the front of the building gives it a very definite presence when seen against its more conservative neighbours. This innovative use of materials roots the building much more firmly to its location.

EVELYN ROAD	G 0-29%	F 30-39%	E 40%	D 41-49%	C 50-59%	B 60-69%	A 70-100%
QUALITATIVE							
Space-Interior						B	
Space-Exterior					C		
Location					C		
Community				D			
QUANTITATIVE							
Construction Cost							A
Cost-rental/purchase						B	
Cost in use					C		
Sustainability				D			
AESTHETICS							
Good Design?							A
Appeal						B	
Innovative?					C		

This table is based on an analytical method of success in contributing to a solution to housing need. The criteria are: Quality of life – does the project maintain or improve good basic standards? Quantitative factors – has the budget achieved the best it can? Aesthetics – does the building work visually?

facing, a rational plan layout was selected, with bedrooms at the rear, away from the road, and living spaces to the front, where the views out over Docklands could be exploited. The layout, with loft-style kitchen/living/dining space, was then enhanced by using higher than normal ceiling heights to maximise the views. In addition, as much built-in storage and furniture as was reasonable was included, the thinking being that,

as this is low-cost/affordable housing, paying for furniture as part of the mortgage package would reduce the expenditure of the prospective owners.

Those eligible as residents for the scheme were selected by the Peabody Trust based on criteria such as income level (single income below £28,500 and double income below £32,500) and field of employment (including public-sector tenants, key workers and those on council housing waiting lists). The

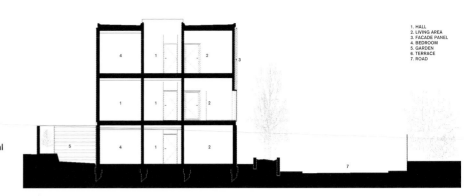

The section takes on the notion of the industrial background of the site. There was previously a tea-crate factory in the area, and the section reflects the idea of stacked cubes.

shared ownership flats start at £210,000 with a share of 30 to 75 per cent for sale. Thus, as an example, a 30 per cent share of a property would cost the purchaser £63,000, and rent would be payable on the remaining 70 per cent.[2]

The exterior cladding was then considered with regard to the ongoing history of the area. The industrial processes have left their distinctive mark, which McLaughlin describes as 'light, sweetness and colour',[3] and in collaboration with lighting artist Martin Richman, radiant light film material was selected for the cladding, or wrapping, of the building instead of the usual brick or timber. This material is coated with colourless metal oxides that disrupt the reflection of light to give an iridescent quality that changes the colour of the walls as you move around the outside of the scheme.

Again, the nature of the history of the site is the generator for the choice of finish for the back and sides. These are clad in timber, but here it has been finished in an industrial grey rather than a more naturalistic colour.

The building is very successful as a small infill project that deals with the particular. Easily erected industrial construction technologies are not only appropriate to the history of the location, but also to the need for keeping costs as low as possible. In the wider context of the Thames Gateway redevelopment, is there a model here that could be utilised to produce affordable housing on a much larger scale?

Of course, timber-frame construction is obvious and will be used, but the attention to the site and how it can drive thinking is very specific. The scale of intervention is what makes the difference. At Silvertown, a small building has been added to the fabric of the area, but the Thames Gateway will be creating new areas for habitation and it is this that requires very careful consideration. Cities are the result of an evolution and have a grain that gives a sense of character and identity. The construction of large swathes of housing can be faceless and soulless, and it is the careful consideration of the particular that has been achieved here that will need to be balanced against the more general problems of building large quantities of homes. Δ+

Notes
1. Press release from Niall McLaughlin Architects, on completion of the project, 2004.
2. Peabody Trust press release, Nicola Millar, Communications Officer, Peabody Trust, 2004.
3. In conversation with the architect, September 2005.

Bruce Stewart is currently researching and writing *The Architects' Navigation Guide to New Housing,* to be published in early 2006 by Wiley-Academy. He trained as an architect and is currently a college teacher at the Bartlett School of Architecture, UCL London.

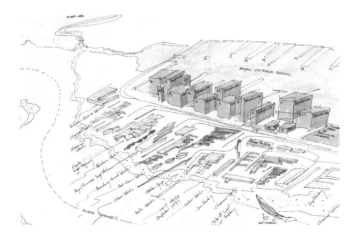

This early sketch by Niall McLaughlin investigates the texture, history and location of the former industrial sites. On the North Woolwich shore, a whale beached herself in 1899 and was subsequently stoned to death by the local workers – a surreal and cruel image. This research into the history of a site is one of the practice's major tools in understanding the projects it undertakes.

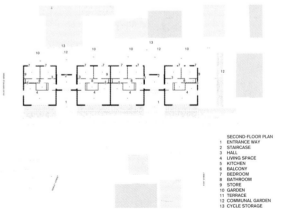

The ground-floor plan shows the rational planning at Evelyn Road. With the major views and higher levels of noise being to the south, it was arranged to place the sleeping accommodation to the rear (the north), with the large open-plan living spaces to the south.

While adhering to the normal perceptions of a square, and conscious of the multifunctional space and the ground, the form continues without separating the roof, wall or floor.

'Springtecture' B

Masaaki Takahashi describes a house, designed by Shuhei Endo, whose coiled corrugated-steel surface seamlessly unifies the inside with the outside, despite its surprisingly rural setting.

Like a scene from a postcard or photo book of Japan, lush and vibrant-green rice fields spread out as far as the eye can see in Shiga prefecture. And rising out of the fields in the middle of this idyllic scene, a giant belt-like structure protrudes from among the orderly rows. That witnesses to this sight do not feel alarmed in the least is quite remarkable: perhaps they think that it is something related to farming or a factory.

Appealing to the Japanese aesthetic, with its twisting curves and narrow edges, it resembles an obi, the belt used on a kimono. On closer examination, one section that extends over a shallow reflection pool makes it apparent that it is not a factory, nor related to farming, but is to be occupied by people.

'Springtecture' B is the creation of Shuhei Endo. The 'B' denotes Biwa, as in Shiga prefecture's Lake Biwa, the largest and most famous in Japan. Equipped with a guesthouse, 'Springtecture' B was built to provide somewhere for local residents to get together. With their cooperation, construction commenced in September 2001 and was completed in May 2002.

Formed of corrugated-steel sheets measuring 90 metres (295 feet) long, 5 metres (16 feet) wide, and 2.7 millimetres (0.1-inch) thick, the metal spirals and reverses course in some areas to create the exterior form. The individual corrugated sheets are secured to each other with bolts in order to maintain structural integrity, and act as an exterior wall (facing interior), a ceiling, an interior wall, a floor, an exterior wall (facing exterior), and as a roof. Thus, the corrugated-steel sheet is the main material for each space.

Endo christened the building 'Springtecture' because of its spiral movement, which resembles a coiled spring. Anticipating the accumulation of heavy winter snow, the belt shape is supported by wide sections and parking areas from within, utilising support posts so that the form does not give way. Inside, seven smaller rooms are partitioned from the main area using brick walls, and the connecting east and west sides have openings with double-paned windows to allow for plenty of light and ventilation. The brick walls were constructed in order to stand parallel to the direction of the spiral, and openings (glazing and polycarbonate) were placed perpendicular to the direction of the spiral for

ventilation and natural light coming from the east and west. The bedroom was finished with 1-millimetre (0.03-inch) thermal insulating paint. This has the same characteristics as 30-millimetre (1.2-inch) polyurethane form. Finished materials of other parts are galvanised corrugated-steel sheets left unpainted.

The entire facility uses radiant floor heating. 'Springtecture' B contains a gallery, conference room, and dining and kitchen area, but the set-up of the entire space is not fixed; rather, it is flexible. In 2004, the design received the 'Surfaces' award at the Venice Biennial's 9th International Architectural Exhibition.

When Endo first utilised corrugated-steel sheeting it was to create Cyclestation M, a town-operated two-storey bicycle parking facility in Shiga. This low-budget project didn't require much decoration or furnishing. However, Endo wanted a structure that

would stand as a symbol of the town and of which the local people could be proud. Taking these requirements into consideration, he created a structure that connected curving corrugated-steel sheets to construct a ceiling and walls. Since then, he has used the same process to create housing with attached shops, offices, an unmanned train station and a variety of other structures.

According to Endo: 'Even when I was younger, I had an interest in traditional carpentry and was attracted to the simple construction of Japanese houses. In university, I studied architecture and was taught that steel-reinforced concrete was the best building material because it is strong and highly fire-resistant. However, concrete construction is always a complicated procedure. Even after completion, though what results is a strong building, it is also very bulky. With wood, it is entirely possible to build

Shuhei Endo, 'Springtecture' B, Shiga prefecture, Japan, 2002
On the southern facade, the corrugated-steel sheeting is wrapped in a spiralling form on an east–west axis, and earthquake-resistant brick walls cover the openings.

The gallery entrance is on the left-hand side, and the conference rooms are on the right, towards the rear.

: small or a large structure with much thinner walls. And corrugated-steel sheets combine the best parts of both materials.'

Western architecture focuses on reductionism and the idea of architecture is separated into interior and exterior. In contrast, Japanese architecture recognises their interdependent relationship. 'When I first used corrugated sheets, I realised that, for me, it was the perfect material through which to express my thoughts on architecture. It's relatively cheap and easy to work with. And almost anyone can use it to capture the simplicity of older Japanese architecture. In addition, when it's no longer needed, it's easy to break down and to move, and it can be also be melted down and reused. It has many of the qualities that are now in demand,' Endo continues.

Minimalism is still popular, and some Japanese architects do not hesitate to build extremely simple, steel box-like houses. Endo points out that most of today's Minimalist architecture is a disguised minimalism – superficial yet remaining in beam-column construction – and that his own architecture goes much beyond this. He proposes new categories and says: 'There are two types of architecture. One is a closed system based only on building concepts, and the other one is an open system, like mine, as you see.'

While he advocates using corrugated steel for construction, he does not support its exclusive use in the case of building smaller houses or spaces to be used by children. Endo believes that using wood and corrugated sheets in construction should be better promoted: 'The origin of the word "architecture" focuses on the technology necessary to separate indoor and outdoor environments. While many people think that it is only the way to focus on creating an indoor area for people, there is really no need to strictly separate them.'

Before Endo, several Japanese architects had supported the use of corrugated steel in building projects, and his own works both reflect the progression of such a material and are organic. However, he realises that corrugated material is not the only material available, so does not hold himself back from exploring. In fact, his interests in building materials have recently drifted towards wood. Seeking new opportunities once again, he is now looking to practise a newly revitalised form of '-tecture'. ᴆ+

Masaaki Takahashi is a Tokyo-based freelance writer and editor, and a regular contributor to ᴆ and *Frame*, amongst others. He is currently working on a new book on young Japanese designers and architects, as well as co-writing a book for Frame Birkhauser. He has recently translated Matilda McQuaid's *Shigeru Ban* into Japanese.

The eastern face. Measuring 5.375 metres (17.6 feet) tall, the impact of the exterior and the changing ceiling height are fascinating features.

Subscribe Now

As an influential and prestigious architectural publication, *Architectural Design* has an almost unrivalled reputation worldwide. Published bimonthly, it successfully combines the currency and topicality of a newsstand magazine with the editorial rigour and design qualities of a book. Consistently at the forefront of cultural thought and design since the 1960s, it has time and again proved provocative and inspirational – an essential catalyst to theoretical, creative and technological advances. Prominent in the 1980s and 1990s for the part it played in Postmodernism and then in Deconstruction, in the 2000s ⌂ has leveraged a depth and level of scrutiny not currently offered elsewhere in the design press. Topics pursued question the outcomes of technical innovations as well as the far-reaching social, cultural and environmental challenges that present themselves today in a period of increasing global uncertainty. ⌂

SUBSCRIPTION RATES 2006
Institutional Rate (Print only or Online only): UK£175/US$290
Institutional Rate (Combined Print and Online): UK£193/US$320
Personal Rate (Print only): UK £99/US$155
Discount Student* Rate (Print only): UK£70/US$110

*Proof of studentship will be required when placing an order. Prices reflect rates for a 2005 subscription and are subject to change without notice.

TO SUBSCRIBE
Phone your credit card order:
+44 (0)1243 843 828

Fax your credit card order to:
+44 (0)1243 770 432

Email your credit card order to:
cs-journals@wiley.co.uk

Post your credit card or cheque order to:
John Wiley & Sons Ltd.
Journals Administration Department
1 Oldlands Way
Bognor Regis
West Sussex PO22 9SA
UK

Please include your postal delivery address with your order.

All ⌂ volumes are available individually. To place an order please write to:
John Wiley & Sons Ltd
Customer Services
1 Oldlands Way
Bognor Regis
West Sussex PO22 9SA

Please quote the ISBN number of the issue(s) you are ordering.

⌂ is available to purchase on both a subscription basis and as individual volumes

○ I wish to subscribe to ⌂ *Architectural Design* at the **Institutional rate of** (Print only or Online only *(delete as applicable)* £175/US$290.

○ I wish to subscribe to ⌂ *Architectural Design* at the **Institutional rate of** (Combined Print and Online) £193/US$320.

○ I wish to subscribe to ⌂ *Architectural Design* at the **Personal rate of £99/US$155.**

○ I wish to subscribe to ⌂ *Architectural Design* at the **Student rate of £70/US$110.**

○ ⌂ *Architectural Design* is available to individuals on either a calendar year or rolling annual basis; Institutional subscriptions are only available on a calendar year basis. Tick this box if you would like your Personal or Student subscription on a rolling annual basis.

Payment enclosed by Cheque/Money order/Drafts.

Value/Currency £/US$ [____]

○ Please charge £/US$ [____] to my credit card.
Account number:
[_ _ _ _ _ _ _ _ _ _ _ _ _ _ _ _ _ _]

Expiry date:
[_ _ _ _ _ _]

Card: Visa/Amex/Mastercard/Eurocard *(delete as applicable)*

Cardholder's signature [____]
Cardholder's name [____]
Address [____]
[____]
[____] Post/Zip Code [____]

Recipient's name [____]
Address [____]
[____]
[____] Post/Zip Code [____]

I would like to buy the following issues at £22.50 each:

○ ⌂ 179 *Manmade Modular Megastructures* Ian Abley + Jonathan Schwinge
○ ⌂ 178 *Sensing the 21st-Century City* Brian McGrath + Grahame Shane
○ ⌂ 177 *The New Mix*, Sara Caples and Everardo Jefferson
○ ⌂ 176 *Design Through Making*, Bob Sheil
○ ⌂ 175 *Food + The City*, Karen A Franck
○ ⌂ 174 *The 1970s Is Here and Now*, Samantha Hardingham
○ ⌂ 173 *4dspace: Interactive Architecture*, Lucy Bullivant
○ ⌂ 172 *Islam + Architecture*, Sabiha Foster
○ ⌂ 171 *Back To School*, Michael Chadwick
○ ⌂ 170 *The Challenge of Suburbia*, Ilka + Andreas Ruby
○ ⌂ 169 *Emergence*, Michael Hensel, Achim Menges + Michael Weinstock
○ ⌂ 168 *Extreme Sites*, Deborah Gans + Claire Weisz
○ ⌂ 167 *Property Development*, David Sokol
○ ⌂ 166 *Club Culture*, Eleanor Curtis
○ ⌂ 165 *Urban Flashes Asia*, Nicholas Boyarsky + Peter Lang
○ ⌂ 164 *Home Front: New Developments in Housing*, Lucy Bullivant
○ ⌂ 163 *Art + Architecture*, Ivan Margolius
○ ⌂ 162 *Surface Consciousness*, Mark Taylor
○ ⌂ 161 *Off the Radar*, Brian Carter + Annette LeCuyer
○ ⌂ 160 *Food + Architecture*, Karen A Franck
○ ⌂ 159 *Versioning in Architecture*, SHoP
○ ⌂ 158 *Furniture + Architecture*, Edwin Heathcote
○ ⌂ 157 *Reflexive Architecture*, Neil Spiller
○ ⌂ 156 *Poetics in Architecture*, Leon van Schaik
○ ⌂ 155 *Contemporary Techniques in Architecture*, Ali Rahim
○ ⌂ 154 *Fame and Architecture*, J Chance and T Schmiedeknecht